THE
NEW YORKER'S
GUIDE TO
LA

THE
ANGELENO'S
GUIDE TO
NYC

THE
NEW YORKER'S
GUIDE TO
LA

THE
ANGELENO'S
GUIDE TO
NYC

HENRY OWENS

RUNNING PRESS
PHILADELPHIA

Running Press
Hachette Book Group
1290 Avenue of the Americas, New York, NY 10104
www.runningpress.com
@Running_Press

Printed in China

First Edition: December 2019

Published by Running Press, an imprint of Perseus Books, LLC, a subsidiary of Hachette Book Group, Inc. The Running Press name and logo is a trademark of the Hachette Book Group.

The Hachette Speakers Bureau provides a wide range of authors for speaking events. To find out more, go to www.hachettespeakersbureau.com or call (866) 376-6591

The publisher is not responsible for websites (or their content) that are not owned by the publisher.

Print book cover and interior design by Jenna McBride

Library of Congress Control Number: 2019943576

ISBNs: 978-0-7624-6689-4 (hardcover), 978-0-7624-6690-0 (ebook)

1010

10 9 8 7 6 5 4 3 2 1

For WB

CONTENTS

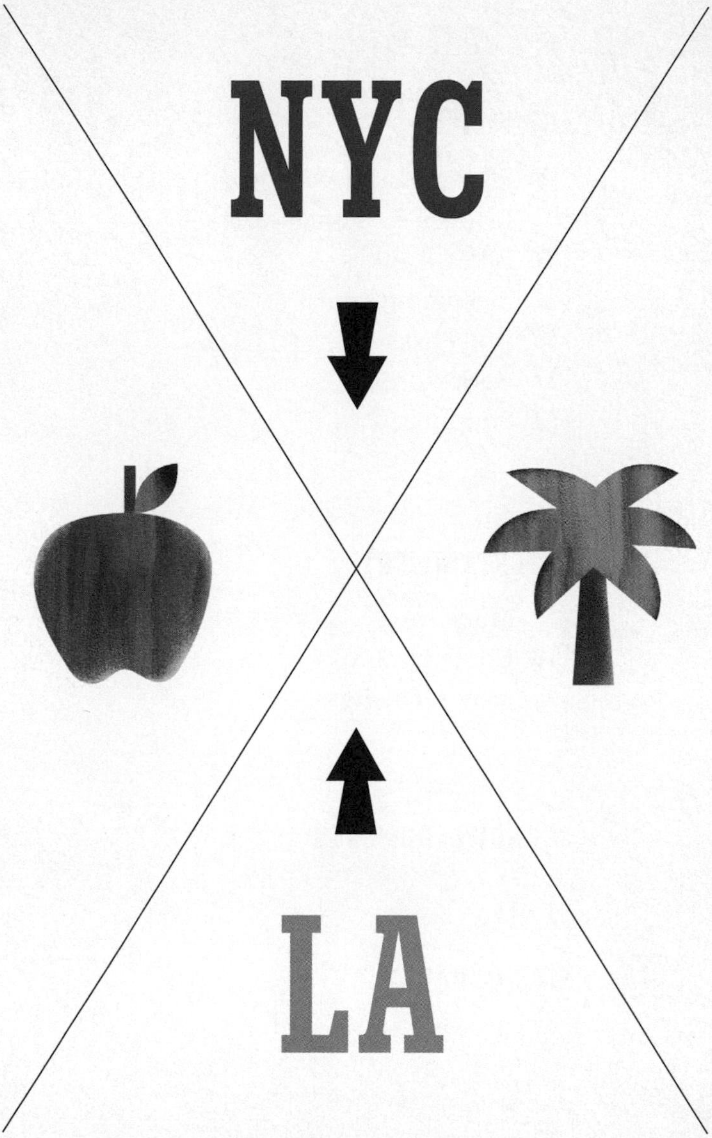
NYC
LA

INTRODUCTION

My friends and I blasted The Strokes in the car as we crept over the George Washington Bridge on my first trip to Manhattan since moving from Los Angeles to attend college on the East Coast. I was a freshman in college and buzzing with excitement at the thought of my first "adult" trip to "The City." The skyscrapers loomed, sounds boomed, and the traffic was terrible. I couldn't comprehend how someone could drive safely through the busy streets of Manhattan. But there we were.

That night, we met up with a few friends and snuck into some bars in Alphabet City. Blocks, streets, avenues, restaurants, neighborhoods—they all blurred together. I was disoriented to say the least.

The next morning, we took the L train out east to Williamsburg to see a vintage clothing store we had heard about. (Apparently, The Strokes shopped there.) As I walked down Bedford, passing a coffee shop and a record store, walking among hipsters in skinny jeans and leather jackets, a thought struck my mind: Williamsburg looked exactly like Silver Lake, the cool Eastside enclave from my native Los Angeles. Suddenly, after a couple of overwhelming, disoriented days, the city started coming into focus.

Williamsburg *is* the Silver Lake of New York.

As I continued to explore New York over the next few days, the one-to-one comparisons started swirling: the posh Upper East Side feels like the celebrity enclave of Beverly Hills; Chelsea is like West Hollywood; Greenwich Village is like Santa Monica; the tourists in Times Square look like those on the Walk of Fame; and on and on and on. Drawing simple comparisons between specific streets, restaurants, sights, and attractions helped orient me in this new place.

Since then, I've come to hear the New York–Los Angeles thing most often stated as a rivalry: It's Letterman versus Leno. It's Biggie versus Tupac. It's the Knicks versus the Lakers; art versus entertainment; Wall Street versus Hollywood. Or it's more general:

No culture in LA!

No space in NYC!

No pizza in LA!

No tacos in NYC!

No walking in LA!

Too much noise in NYC!

No one reads in LA!

No one relaxes
in NYC!

No seasons in LA!

Terrible weather
in NYC!

Everyone's lazy in LA!

Everyone's neurotic
in NYC!

Nothing's open past
10:00 p.m. in LA!

No one's awake
before 10:00 a.m.
in NYC!

But really, it's a pointless debate. Instead, it's these dichotomies that make both places so great.

Sure, we all know New York doesn't have tacos quite like those in Los Angeles . . . but New York has way better pizza. Of course Los Angeles doesn't have Central Park, but it does have miles of amazing beaches. By thinking about these one-to-ones more carefully, you can understand each city better—and maybe even learn to love each in its own way.

That's how we arrived at this book. It's a travel guide for any Angeleno heading east or any New Yorker looking west. It's a tool for anyone new to either city. It's an overview, a glimpse, a taste of two cities—all from one guy's point of view (with a lot of input from many opinionated friends on each coast).

You might think of it as a comparative atlas that'll at once orient newbies to the particulars of a new coast and also introduce diehards on either side to find something admirable on the opposite coast.

Maybe you're hankering for Apple Pan while in NYC. This book will point you to the equivalent burger. (Hint: it's at Corner Bistro.) Or maybe you're desperate for some modern art, but you feel stranded out in LA. (Why don't you check out the Broad?) Need your pizza fix while in LA or your taco fix while in NYC? Wondering what to do in NYC if you love hiking on Runyon, or where to catch an indie flick in LA when you're away from your beloved Angelika? Flip through this book's pages for one-to-one comparisons and side-by-side explanations as well as tips, tricks, and guidance on these quintessential American opposites.

This is, after all, the Angeleno's guide to New York *and* the New Yorker's guide to Los Angeles. It's a "comparative travel guide," like an English–to–foreign language dictionary for the best two cities on the planet.

With neighborhood overviews and guides on food, art, music, shopping, transportation, and outings, this book will not only explain how to navigate and survive the opposite coast, but also how to thrive there.

NEW YORK AND LOS ANGELES:

🍎🌴🍎🌴🍎🌴	NEW YORK	LOS ANGELES
POPULATION	8.6 million	4 million
SIZE	302.64 square miles	468.67 square miles
YEAR FOUNDED	Incorporated 1624	Incorporated 1850
LANGUAGES SPOKEN	Approx. 800	Approx. 225
NO. OF TREES	5.2 million	10 million
NO. OF AIRPORTS	5 (JFK, LGA, EWR, ISP, HPN)	5 (LAX, ONT, SNA, BUR, LGB)
NO. OF RESTAURANTS	Approximately 8,282	Approximately 8,500
NO. OF HOTEL ROOMS	107,000+	98,600+
AVG. HIGH TEMP IN JAN.	39°F	68°F
AVERAGE SNOWFALL	2–3 feet	0 inches
PERCENTAGE OF POP. OVER 25 WITH HIGH SCHOOL DIPOLOMA	81%	76.4%
PERCENTAGE OF POP. OVER 25 WITH COLLEGE DEGREE	36.7%	33%

BY THE NUMBERS

	NEW YORK	LOS ANGELES
AVERAGE TRAVEL TIME TO WORK	40.8 minutes	30.9 minutes
PERCENTAGE OF POP. THAT'S FOREIGN BORN	37.6%	37.2%
TALLEST BUILDING	One World Trade at 1,776 feet	Wilshire Grand Center at 1,099 feet
MEDIAN HOUSEHOLD INCOME	$57,782	$54,501
POPULATION PER SQUARE MILE	27,012.5	8,092.3
MOST POPULAR BABY NAMES (2017)	Liam & Olivia	Noah & Emma
U.S. PRESIDENTS WHO WERE BORN IN THE CITY	Teddy Roosevelt & Donald Trump (plus three more from the state: Franklin D. Roosevelt, Millard Fillmore & Martin Van Buren)	None (but Richard Nixon hails from Yorba Linda, California, a suburb in Orange County)

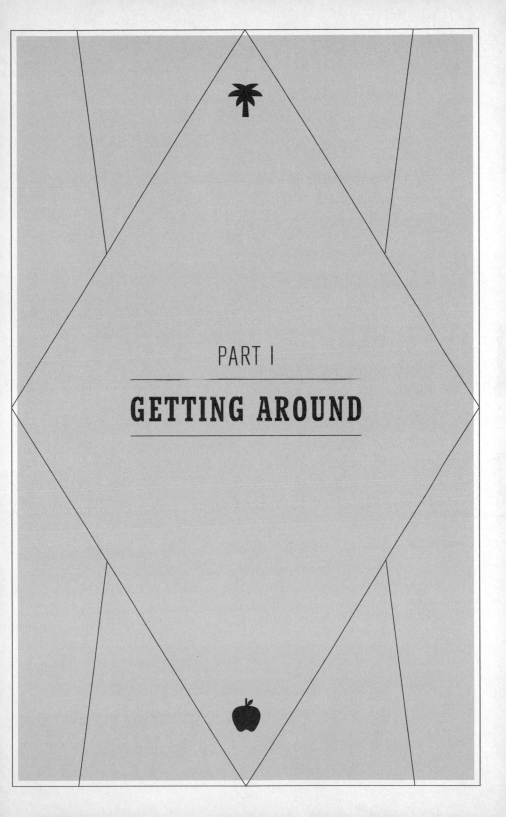

PART I

GETTING AROUND

TRANSPORTATION

Perhaps no aspect of either city defines its character more than how its denizens get from A to B.

Everybody walks in New York

Everybody drives in Los Angeles

It's exercise versus A/C

Convenience of public transportation versus the comfort of your own car

So, how can you begin to compare the two? How can a New Yorker find her way in Los Angeles? How will an Angeleno know what train to take in New York?

"I WAS BORN THE DAY I GOT MY LICENSE."

—Jay Leno

THE LAY OF THE LAND

First things first, it's important to understand the basic geography of each city.

New York is famous for its grid system: Avenues divide the town like columns and streets intersect it like rows. It's easy to remember and simple to navigate.

Los Angeles also has a grid of its very own—just one with more to remember. Mastering it will vastly improve your enjoyment and understanding of the city.

> ### "I'M AN L.A. GUY. I DRIVE. I AM MY TRUCK. MY TRUCK IS ME."
>
> —Jonathan Gold

Begin with the major freeways:

The 10 cuts straight across town from the beach on the West Coast past downtown to the east. The 405 intersects the 10, drawing a line between West LA and, well, everything else, running north from the San Fernando Valley all the way down to Irvine in the south.

Following the 10 eastbound, you'll reach the 101, which wraps around downtown to separate Hollywood from Silver Lake before snaking over the Hills and carving a path through the Valley—from Studio City through Sherman Oaks, Encino, Tarzana, Woodland Hills, and Calabasas all the way up to Ventura County and straight out of town. Okay, so it's not quite as simple as First, Second, Third, Lexington, Park, Madison . . . but it's a start.

The major boulevards of Los Angeles can also provide a useful grid to the city. Each runs from the ocean to downtown. From the Hills in the north progressing south, you have:

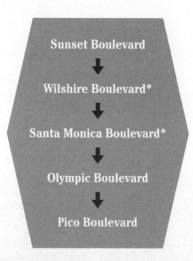

Sunset Boulevard
⬇
Wilshire Boulevard*
⬇
Santa Monica Boulevard*
⬇
Olympic Boulevard
⬇
Pico Boulevard

*Note: Wilshire and Santa Monica cross in Beverly Hills.

RULES OF THUMB

Twenty city blocks in NYC equals one mile.	It takes twenty minutes to drive anywhere in LA. (Even if it's one mile away.)
New York has the subway.	Los Angeles has valet.
New York's "across town" means going east or west.	Los Angeles's "across town" means crossing the 405.
New Yorkers always specify an address by street and then avenue (as in, "the corner of Twenty-Third and Fifth," for Twenty-Third Street and Fifth Avenue).	Angelenos say "the" in front of every freeway name—and refer to them by their number, rather than name. (It's the 405, the 101, the 10.)
New York has highways— for which you pay tolls.	In LA, at least it's free to sit hours on end in traffic.
New York has Citi Bike.	Los Angeles has Bird scooters. And the weather for them.

"DRIVING A BENTLEY TO TARGET—ONLY IN LA DOES THIS MAKE SENSE."

—A. M. Homes, *This Book Will Save Your Life*

NAVIGATING

Now, how to get around these grids?

The 4/5/6 train and the A/C/E train are like Sunset and Olympic Boulevards. Each provides a straight shot to traverse the city.

The 4/5/6 runs north-south along the East Side of Manhattan, while the A/C/E runs north-south along the West Side. In Los Angeles, Sunset and Olympic both run from the beach to downtown, with Sunset being the farthest north before the Hills and Olympic a bit farther south.

Find either of these main subway lines or boulevards, hop on, and you'll find an easy path to traverse the city. That is, assuming everything's running smoothly. New York's "train delays"—the catchall term for the subways' inevitable route changes and irregular intervals due to construction, inclement weather, maintenance, and, unfortunately, jumpers—are like "traffic" in Los Angeles, which never seems to cease.

If you want to circumvent the main drag or avoid these woes?

> "I LIKE TO WATCH PEOPLE. SOMETIMES I RIDE THE SUBWAY ALL DAY AND LOOK AT THEM AND LISTEN TO THEM. I JUST WANT TO FIGURE OUT WHO THEY ARE AND WHAT THEY WANT AND WHERE THEY'RE GOING."

—Ray Bradbury

For starters, in Los Angeles, never ever—seriously, *never*—drive east to west (or west to east) during rush hour, generally between about 4:30 and 7:00 p.m. on weekdays. You'll get caught in insanely long lines on any avenue approaching the 405 for miles in either direction. Make plans to stay local accordingly.

In New York, check Twitter for train delays and always have a backup plan. Check the map and figure out which alternate train will get you close enough—and then walk the rest. And to that end: If you're less than one mile away (or less than two stops) from your destination, just walk.

> "IN LA PEOPLE DON'T HAVE TIME TO STOP; ANYWHERE THEY HAVE TO GO THEY GO THERE IN A CAR. THE POOREST MAN HAS A CAR IN LOS ANGELES; HE MIGHT NOT HAVE A ROOF OVER HIS HEAD BUT HE HAS A CAR. AND HE KNOWS WHERE HE'S GOING TOO."

—Walter Mosley, *Devil in a Blue Dress*

NEIGHBORHOODS

How do you begin to understand and navigate the two largest cities in America? The best way to tackle it—to make it more manageable—is by breaking it down into sections or, well, neighborhoods.

But even that can be formidable. While NYC has fifty-nine official "community districts," it has, by some accounts, up to three hundred distinct neighborhoods. The *Los Angeles Times*' similarly divides LA into 272 distinct neighborhoods—while writer Eric Brightwell created an incredible map of more than 472 clearly defined and distinct neighborhoods in Los Angeles. Needless to say, the borders between neighborhoods aren't so clearly drawn—and can evolve over time.

One reason for the complexity is that neighborhoods can be defined by such a broad set of criteria—from their ethnic and cultural histories to their physical and geographical boundaries, from the lines drawn by real estate developers to the restrictions set by city planners. On top of that, the people who live and work in any given neighborhood are constantly changing.

"MOST CITIES ARE NOUNS. NEW YORK'S A VERB."

—John F. Kennedy

> ### "LOS ANGELES IS A LARGE CITY-LIKE AREA SURROUNDING THE BEVERLY HILLS HOTEL."

—Fran Lebowitz

Even still, New York and Los Angeles both have plenty of iconic neighborhoods that are famous in their own right, such as Beverly Hills, Greenwich Village, Compton, Washington Heights, Williamsburg, and Silverlake, just as a few examples. And often the simplest way to understand where you are is by pointing to a similar place in very broad terms: You're shopping on Lexington, and you might as well be on Rodeo Drive; you're strolling along Bleeker, and you have flashes of Abbot Kinney; you're jaunting down Bedford, and you feel like you're on Sunset.

So, let's dive into these two massive cities by exploring a sampling of its popular neighborhoods in side-by-side comparisons.

NEW YORK CITY

WASHINGTON HEIGHTS

THE BRONX

HARLEM

UPPER WEST SIDE

ASTORIA

UPPER EAST SIDE

MIDTOWN

CHELSEA

LONG ISLAND CITY

QUEENS

SOHO

WILLIAMSBURG

COBBLE HILL

FORT GREENE

LOS ANGELES

BURBANK

STUDIO CITY

LOS FELIZ

BEVERLY HILLS

SUNSET STRIP

HOLLYWOOD

SILVERLAKE

BRENTWOOD

RODEO DR 400

WEST HOLLYWOOD

CHINATOWN

SANTA MONICA

WEST ADAMS

CRENSHAW

INGLEWOOD

EL SEGUNDO

> "THE TRUE NEW YORKER SECRETLY BELIEVES
> THAT PEOPLE LIVING ANYWHERE ELSE
> HAVE TO BE, IN SOME SENSE, KIDDING."

—John Updike

> "LOS ANGELES IS 72 SUBURBS IN
> SEARCH OF A CITY."

—Dorothy Parker

SOHO ⟷ SANTA MONICA

Can a neighborhood be cool and cliché at the same time?

SoHo and Santa Monica both exude a hip vibe that's cool, expensive, artsy,

> **Formerly artist-dominated, now somehow chic while still overrun by tourists.**

and young—yet somehow both neighborhoods overflow with tourists. It's not that these out-of-towners have ruined the areas; it's just that they're there in droves, and businesses have popped up among more local fare to cater to their tastes.

DID YOU KNOW?

SoHo stands for "South of Houston," a term coined in 1962 that refers to the neighborhood's location below Houston Street, a main east-west thoroughfare in lower Manhattan.

DID YOU KNOW?

Santa Monica is technically its own city separate from Los Angeles, with its own school system, police force, and mayor. It's up against Pacific Ocean and otherwise surrounded entirely by LA.

CHELSEA ⟷ WEST HOLLYWOOD

Cultural and LGBTQ hubs. Chelsea has the Hotel Chelsea and West Hollywood has the Chateau Marmont.*

The Chelsea opened its doors in 1884 in what was at the time the center of the Manhattan theater district. Since the beginning of the twentieth century, it has been a beacon for cutting-edge artists, musicians, and writers, playing host to the likes of Madonna, Robert Mapplethorpe, Julian Schnabel, Yves Klein, Diego Rivera, Leonard Cohen, and Janis Joplin. The famous Warhol film *Chelsea Girls* takes place there, and Sid Vicious was accused of murdering his girlfriend Nancy Spungen within its halls. Allen Ginsberg and Arthur Miller lived and wrote at the famed residence.

On the opposite coast, the Chateau opened its doors in 1929, quickly attracting the coolest artists of its day and maintaining that status ever since. To list of celebrities who've stayed within its private bungalows would be pointless—who hasn't been to the Chateau? Needless to say, anyone who's anyone has stayed or—at the very least—partied there.

The two hotels say a lot about the neighborhoods as a whole: colorful and eclectic, twisted and weird, but with no shortage of high-class residents, visitors, or wealth.

*Technically, the Chateau Marmont falls outside the official limits of West Hollywood—yet the official boundary for WeHo's literally across the street!

DID YOU KNOW?

In 1984, mainly as a result of the campaigning by many of its LGBTQ residents, West Hollywood became its own city. The region—and now city—has long been one of the foremost gay enclaves in the country and includes the famed Sunset Strip, with its own particular brand of nightlife, as well as the stretch of Santa Monica Boulevard east of Doheny and famous for its gay clubs. As a result of its top-notch nightlife, walkability, and trendy restaurants, the area also attracts countless postgrads and twentysomethings.

SOME PEOPLE CALL IT WEHO FOR SHORT

UPPER EAST SIDE ⟷ BEVERLY HILLS

Iconic. Is there a neighborhood more iconic than Beverly Hills? It's featured in countless TV shows (*90210*, *The Beverly Hillbillies*) and movies (*Beverly Hills Cop*, *Troop Beverly Hills*), but perhaps Weezer put it best, singing simply:

> ## "THAT'S WHERE I WANNA BE."

The Upper East Side has the Metropolitan Museum of Art, the Guggenheim, shopping, and glorious townhomes lining Central Park. And with these monuments, it might be just as iconic as Beverly Hills.

DID YOU KNOW?

Beverly Hills is technically its own city separate from that of LA. While 90210 might be the most famous zip code, the city has four more of its very own: 90209, 90211, 90212, and 90213.

Can there be an area in the nation more jam-packed with cultural icons and institutions than Midtown Manhattan?

> **Tourist attractions, entertainment capitals.**

Hollywood, of course, has its iconic white block-letter sign, perched high in the hills like a crown on the city's head, but its other institutions—Capital Records, the Walk of Fame, the Chinese Theatre—don't really compete. Yet is there a neighborhood the world over more iconic in and of itself than Hollywood?

It may be the world capital of the entertainment industry, but these days it has mostly become a place to exploit its own image, a mecca for tourists to spot the sign, see the Walk of Fame, and snap a picture with a random dude in a Spider-Man costume.

You'll find the same in the unofficial capital of Midtown, Times Square. Little needs to be said about Times Square, the "Crossroads of the World," one of the most visited tourist destinations on the planet. Broadway, billboards, shopping, the New Years' Eve ball drop. With millions of tourists visiting each neighborhood every year, there must be something special about both.

UPPER WEST SIDE ⟷ BRENTWOOD

Beautiful. The Upper West Side and Brentwood both feature some of the nicest, most bucolic, idyllic homes in the country. Unmatched views of Central Park in ornate prewar buildings and private gated hideaways with unmatched proximity to the Pacific Ocean, respectively.

Central Park West in particular, the avenue running alongside Central Park on the Westside, features some of the most extraordinary homes in the city—no, the country—including, for example, the famed Dakota building in which John Lennon famously lived before his untimely death. The Upper West Side, in general, features incredible architecture and truly grand residential buildings. It's also a cultural hub with Lincoln Center and the American Museum of Natural History all calling it home.

Brentwood is an exclusive and gorgeous enclave of LA, and from a geographical standpoint, the counterpart to Central Park West might be the tree-lined San Vicente Boulevard, which runs about five miles from the 405 to the beach, with a wide, grassy median spotted with large coral trees.

WILLIAMSBURG ↔ SILVERLAKE

Where do young hipsters flee when rents sky-rocket? East.

Hipster havens.

It's true in both cities. In Los Angeles, it's Silver Lake, east of the 101. In New York, it's Williamsburg, the land east of the East River. Both regions are beacons for artists and musicians (read: baristas and bartenders) seeking cheaper rent and displacing many of the minority communities that have long lived there. (Los Angeles's Eastside has long been home to a thriving Latino population, while New York's Williamsburg has a large Jewish Hasidic community.) As news spread throughout the early aughts of the creative boom taking place on each east side, entrepreneurs, developers, and restaurateurs quickly chased the opportunity.

The heart of Williamsburg can be found at the corner of North Seventh Street and Bedford Avenue, the site of the first L train stop in Brooklyn. And in Los Angeles, you'd say the same about the intersection of Santa Monica and Sunset Boulevards, known as Sunset Junction. From there, you can explore Williamsburg by strolling south on Bedford, and in Silver Lake, walking south on Sunset to find your fill of overpriced espresso, vintage clothes, handmade jewelry, home goods shops, and artisanal everything.

Waterviews can be found by strolling along the East River in Williamsburg, while the approximately two-mile loop round the Silver Lake Reservoir can provide the same out west.

Seek out either neighborhood for great people watching, good food, and a millennial-heavy vibe.

WASHINGTON HEIGHTS ↔ WEST ADAMS

Rich history, youthful future. One of the oldest sections of Los Angeles, West Adams has an outstanding collection of historic buildings and Victorian homes and has been an enclave for wealthy African American residents since the turn of the century. As the ugly segregationist policies of Beverly Hills in its early years prevented black families from moving there, West Adams attracted many of the city's celebrities such as Ray Charles, Joe Lewis, and Little Richard. The neighborhood has also amassed an incredible cultural history through landmarks like Paul Williams–designed Golden State Mutual Life Insurance Company Building, which once housed the nation's largest black-owned insurance agency. The neighborhood borders—and some say overlaps with—Baldwin Hills, commonly referred to as the "black Beverly Hills," and a new wave of young people have recently flocked to and flourished in the neighborhood.

On the opposite coast, Washington Heights was dubbed "the new Williamsburg," by a *New York Post* article in the summer of 2019. Millennials flocked to the outer boroughs in the early-aughts, making places like Williamsburg hipster capitals, but the effect has gone full circle: rents in those areas are now higher than in Manhattan. Young people, as a result, started moving back to Manhattan, seeking out the slightly cheaper rents in Washington Heights.

The influx of millennials—and the hip business that cater to them—has added to the already deeply rich and diverse history of the neighborhood. Since the middle of the twentieth century, Dominican immigrants have made the neighborhood their home, and by at least the 1980s, it became one of the largest Dominican centers in the United States. In more recent years, the neighborhood got widespread fame from the breakout sensation of Lin-Manuel Miranda's first musical, *In the Heights*. He grew up in and is still a resident of the neighborhood. The area features lots of parks and green spaces and the incredibly charming little red lighthouse perched under the George Washington Bridge.

Charming hideaways. When you picture Brooklyn, do you envision rows of brownstone buildings along tree-lined streets with happy couples pushing strollers past bustling independent coffee shops and bookstores? If so, you're picturing Cobble Hill.

The Cobble Hill enclave sits just below Brooklyn Heights—the historically wealthy and exclusive neighborhood along the promenade overlooking downtown Manhattan—and oozes nearly as much old-world charm as its more expensive neighbor. The rows of brownstone town houses that give it its quintessentially "Brooklyn"—and picturesque—vibe have survived mainly untouched to this day due to intense conservation efforts that started in the late 1950s. The neighborhood hasn't always been such a hot spot, but in the postwar years, young professionals started to flock back to Brooklyn

> ## "NEW YORK CITY IS THE PLACE WHERE THEY SAID: HEY BABE, TAKE A WALK ON THE WILD SIDE."

—"Walk on the Wild Side" by Lou Reed

as an alternative to the farther-out suburbs, seeking bargains for brownstones in an area not so far away. In 1959, the Cobble Hill Association was created to protect the charm of the neighborhood and stop high-rises from popping up, and six years later, the little fairytale park was created in the center of the neighborhood.

> # "FROM HOLLYWOOD AND VINE TO THE SUNSET STRIP, THERE'S SO MUCH GOIN' ON, YOU CAN LOSE YOUR GRIP."

—"Back in LA" by B.B. King

Today, it's a hot spot for well-to-do young families, successful creative types, and a handful of celebrities.

The Los Feliz neighborhood of Los Angeles likewise feels like a quaint little town somehow smacked up alongside the craziness of Hollywood. It rests at the base of Griffith Park—a massive urban park that's about five times the size of Central Park—that gives it a sort of rustic feel. It has its fair share of authentic Spanish-style cottages and homes, a legacy from its original days as a rancho, which were traditional land grants of prime farm space given by the Spanish and then Mexican governments from the 1780s through the 1840s. It also features many epic mansions in the Laughlin Park section, which has been called the "showrunners' corner" of the city and is one of the toniest neighborhoods in all of LA. To top off the charm, it also features the quirky Shakespeare Bridge—a fairy tale–like bridge along Franklin Avenue—and Walt Disney's first home in the city.

HAMPTONS ⟷ MALIBU

Even the rich and famous need a break sometimes. So where do they run to steal a long weekend by the beach? The Hamptons in New York and Malibu in Los Angeles.

The Hamptons refers to a stretch of villages along the southeastern coast of Long Island, beginning with Eastport and ending at the farthest tip in Montauk. It's mainly old farming land, so the landscape features wide open and lush greenery up against long, calm beaches. Millionaires and billionaires spend summer weekends here, relaxing by oversize pools, sunbathing at the beach, and dining out at overpriced restaurants to see and be seen.

Malibu is the sliver of coast north of Santa Monica and Los Angeles, running up for twenty-some-odd miles to Ventura County. It's a paradise within paradise and somewhat a land of contradictions. Surfrider Beach—among the most popular surf spots in the world and a hub for beach bums and stoned surfer dudes—exists just minutes from mansions worth well into the tens of millions of dollars.

SANTA CATALINA ISLAND ⟷ CONEY ISLAND

Want to escape the city to a bygone era? Sure, you can drive up north to the Catskills from NYC to get some peace and quiet in nature or drive up north to Ojai from LA for the same. But that's so boring. Instead, take a quick trek out to two islands that feature throwback culture and kitschy charm: Santa Catalina Island and Coney Island.

William Wrigley Jr., the famous chewing gum tycoon, bought a controlling stake in the tiny Catalina Island only twenty-six miles off the coast of Long Beach in 1919 and set off to build a glamorous getaway from Hollywood. By 1929, the Casino opened its doors, which, despite its name, featured no gambling, but did feature the first-ever theater specifically designed to play movies with sound (or "talkies"). The cinema became a frequent destination for Cecil B. DeMille, Louis B. Mayer, and Samuel Goldwyn throughout the '30s—and a popular tourist destination throughout the middle of the century.

Around the same time, Coney Island was a super popular beach getaway for folks from New York. Just fourteen miles from Grand Central, Coney Island features the mystique of a beach resort while still being easily accessible. In 1916, Nathan Handwerker started serving hot dogs along the boardwalk, and the now-famous wooden roller coaster, the Cyclone, opened in 1927. From the late 1880s to World War II, Coney Island was the largest amusement area in the United States. Now, it's undergone a resurgence in popularity again, welcoming millions of visitors a year.

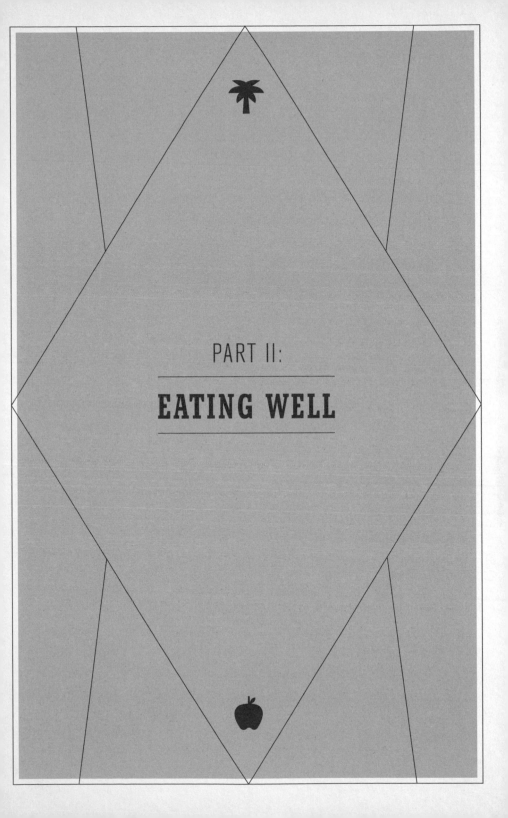

PART II:

EATING WELL

What better way to understand a place than by its cuisine? Sure, there has been plenty of rivalries as to which one does what better—no bagels in LA! no tacos in NY!—but there's one thing for sure: both cities have incredibly diverse populations that have produced endlessly fascinating cuisines. So, let's dive in and check out the best of both worlds and look at some comparisons to satiate you on either coast.

PIZZA & TACOS

New Yorkers famously begrudge the fact that they can't find a decent slice of pizza in LA, while Angelenos love to complain about the dearth of decent tacos in NY. But really, they're similar: Each food is an outrageously delicious, handheld, and inexpensive snack (or meal) that epitomizes its city. So why fight about it? You ought to embrace the best of either world.

New York pizza first came of age at the turn of the century when an Italian immigrant named Gennaro Lombardi opened a grocery store in Little Italy. Some say the famous "pizza by the slice" method emerged when an employee of his, Antonio Totonno Pero, started cooking oversize pies like those from their native Naples, allowing customers the ability to offer whatever money they had in exchange for a corresponding amount of the pie.

Cielito Lindo Food Stand has stood on Olvera Street in the historic Mexican center of downtown Los Angeles since the 1930s, serving deep-fried rolled taquitos that food historian Gustavo Arellano has deemed the "Plymouth Rock of tacos." From there, tacos spread like wildfire across Southern California, being sold by illegal street vendors, Mexican American-owned diners, and authentic Mexican restaurants alike. For the next thirty years, the taco solidified itself as a Los Angeles food staple. In 1962, a restaurateur named Glen Bell introduced the delicacy to his burger stand in San Bernardino. He renamed his establishment Taco Tia and it quickly expanded, eventually becoming Taco Bell and introducing the rest of the nation to the fast-casual taco. Since then, taco spots have continued to spring up and thrive across the expansive city.

Bottom line? You're eating a piece of NYC or LA history, whether you eat a slice of pizza or a taco.

BEST PIZZA

*33 Havemeyer Street,
Brooklyn, NY 11211*

Frank Pinello's 2010
Brooklyn hot spot revives
an old-school tradition
in a hip neighborhood.

TITO'S TACOS

*11222 Washington Place,
Culver City, CA 90230*

This legendary Culver
City staple—with crunchy
shells, cold cheese, and
ground mystery meat—
is not for everyone, but
has a dedicated following.

JOE'S PIZZA

*7 Carmine Street,
New York, NY 10014*

Quintessential simple,
plain cheese pizza since
1974—and for around
$3 a slice.

TACOS POR FAVOR

*1408 Olympic Boulevard,
Santa Monica, CA 90404*

Classic Southern California
Mexican restaurant with
a full menu and out-
standing tacos.

JOHN'S BRICK OVEN PIZZA

*278 Bleecker Street,
New York, NY 10014*

Nearly ninety-year-old
Greenwich Village institution famous for its garlic.

LEO'S TACOS TRUCK

*1515 S La Brea Avenue,
Los Angeles, CA 90019*

Beyond belief, succulent
al pastor (pork) served off
a giant rotisserie in a truck
permanently parked in a
gas station.

ROBERTA'S

261 Moore Street,
Brooklyn, NY 11206

A rumored favorite of Jay-Z and Beyoncé and an emblem of the increasingly hip Bushwick enclave of Brooklyn with wait times as outrageous as its pizza.

RICKY'S FISH TACOS

3061 Riverside Drive,
Los Angeles, CA 90039

The quintessential fried-fish taco made famous by Los Angeles's Eastside.

GRIMALDI'S

1 Front Street,
Brooklyn, NY 11201

Longtime waterfront staple with thin crust and long lines that move mystifyingly fast.

MARISCOS JALISCO

3040 E Olympic Boulevard,
Los Angeles, CA 90023

Widely regarded as the best fish tacos in the region.

LUCALI

575 Henry Street,
Brooklyn, NY 11231

Intimate Carroll Gardens hideaway with outstanding pies.

B.S. TAQUERIA

514 W Seventh Street,
Los Angeles, CA 90014

High-end, but authentic.

> **"I WOULD FLY TO LOS ANGELES JUST FOR A CHEESEBURGER WITH PICKLES AND EXTRA TOMATOES FROM IN-N-OUT."**
>
> —Zoë Kravitz

> **"MAN WHO INVENTED THE HAMBURGER WAS SMART; MAN WHO INVENTED THE CHEESEBURGER WAS A GENIUS."**
>
> —Matthew McConaughey

BURGERS

Los Angeles has long been thought of as the better burger town over New York, in large part due to In-N-Out. However, with the rise of Shake Shack and the high-end offerings from steak house staples like Peter Luger, New York has emerged as a great burger city in its own right.

In 1940, Richard and Maurice McDonald pioneered the fast-food burger operation in Southern California. Eight years later, Harry and Esther Snyder opened the first In-N-Out Burger in Baldwin Park, part of greater Los Angeles. And ever since, the simple hamburger has become synonymous with the region, with fans ranging from Gordon Ramsay (who ordered two double-doubles on his first visit) to Thomas Keller of the famed French Laundry to Julia Child to Anthony Bourdain (who once famously called it the best restaurant in Los Angeles). Despite its popularity for more than seventy years and its remarkable success, In-N-Out refuses to expand beyond the western United States. With an insistence on fresh ingredients (neither a freezer nor a 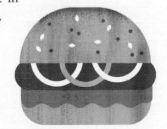 microwave has ever been used on any of its premises), an expansion beyond the West would be impossible without changing its food sources and distribution chain.

Despite a lack of great fast food options, New York has long been known as having some of the best steaks in the nation, so it follows that the city also has some of the best meat to make some truly great burgers. Take, for example, the legendary steak house Peter Luger and its burger made of prime-grade chuck and the dry-aged trimmings from its famous porterhouses. It's a treat that's only served at lunchtime on weekdays, and it's a very different experience from the russian dressing, er, I mean "Secret Sauce" slathered on the thin patty of In-N-Out.

Here's your comparative guide to the burgers on either coast.

NEW YORK	LOS ANGELES
SHAKE SHACK	**IN-N-OUT**
Multiple locations	*Multiple locations*
Famed restaurateur Danny Meyer's successful swing at a no-frills fast-food joint with exceptionally high-quality meat.	The classic, delicious fast-food hamburger with a menu that hasn't changed since 1948.
CORNER BISTRO	**APPLE PAN**
331 West Fourth Street, New York, NY 10014	*10801 W Pico Boulevard, Los Angeles, CA 90064*
Old-school charm and a basic menu calls to mind an earlier time.	A single wrap-around counter, no plates, no utensils, no problem— just simple goodness since 1947.

MINETTA TAVERN

113 MacDougal Street,
New York, NY 10012

Downtown high-end steak
house with a crowded,
vintage French bistro vibe
that serves an over-the-top
juicy burger.

FATHER'S OFFICE

1018 Montana Avenue,
Santa Monica, CA 90403

Cramped with classy
1950s style decor, they
serve a succulent blue-
cheese burger—with no
modifications allowed.

BURGER JOINT

Inside Le Parker
Meridien Hotel,
119 W Fifty-Sixth Street,
New York, NY 10019

A lesson in contradiction,
this wooded and graffiti-
strewn dive sits hidden
behind the posh lobby of
an upscale hotel, serving
classically simple burgers
and delicious fries.

CASSELL'S HAMBURGERS

Hotel Normandie,
3600 W Sixth Street,
Los Angeles, CA 90020

A staple since 1948,
serving simple premium
beef without distraction
inside the lobby of a
historic Koreatown hotel.

J. G. MELON

1291 Third Ave,
New York, NY 10021

Simple burgers in a dimly
lit, pretense-free bar. It's
a staple of the Upper East
Side and home to one of the
city's reliably best burgers.

PIE 'N BURGER

913 E California Blvd,
Pasadena, CA 91106

It continues to serve its
simple classic the same
way since 1963, making
it an evergreen legend
across all of LA.

DELIS

German immigrants brought a food market for meat and cheese called a *delikatessen* to New York. Soon afterward, Jewish immigrants—many from Germany and surrounding regions—brought over kosher traditions evolving the traditional delis.

It's theorized that due to kosher rules dictating the separation of dairy and meat—with fish being allowed to be served alongside dairy (i.e., butter and cream cheese)—that over the course of the next few decades, the original delikatessens started to divide into two categories: meat-focused stores, known as *delis*, and fish-focused stores, known as *appetizing shops*. It's the children of these Jewish immigrants who opened the famous wave of delis and appetizing shops across the city that have become New York stalwarts, such as the still-standing Katz's on the Lower East Side.

On the opposite coast, as the movie industry boomed and Jewish Americans flocked to the city, Los Angeles's own crop of delis started to take hold.

> ## "DADDY, HOW COME IN KANSAS CITY THE BAGELS TASTE LIKE JUST ROUND BREAD?"
>
> —Calvin Trillin

WHAT BAGEL DEBATE?

What's more New York than a bagel?

Even with its own batch of fantastic delis, Los Angeles could never quite master the bagel. Some have said it's the water—that New York water provides a magical composition of minerals that make its bagels so fluffy and chewy—and Larry King even capitalized on this theory by opening the Original Brooklyn Water Bagel Co. in Beverly Hills. And to be fair, there's a good many shops across the city with perfectly edible bagels . . . but to try and compare them to New York's feels silly.

As trends in dining have ebbed and flowed over the years, the deli and appetizing shops in both New York and Los Angeles have remained evergreen in popularity, quality, and iconography. And in recent years a new batch of chefs has cropped up, innovating on these past traditions and bringing a newfound energy to the art of Jewish cooking at places like Sadelle's in New York and Wexler's in Los Angeles.

Here's a roundup of some one-to-one comparisons.

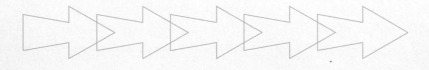

BARNEY GREENGRASS

*541 Amsterdam Avenue,
New York, NY 10024*

Originally founded in
Harlem in 1908, Barney
Greengrass moved his
fine foods store to its
current location in the
Upper West Side in 1929,
and it's been an iconic
institution ever since.

NATE 'N AL'S

*414 N Beverly Drive,
Beverly Hills, CA 90210*

Founded in 1945, this is
a celebrity hot spot and
Beverly Hills mainstay
that's as iconic for its
famous customers as it
is for its food.

LIEBMAN'S KOSHER DELI

*552 W 235th Street,
Bronx, NY 10463*

This Bronx legend is still
run by the family that
founded it in 1953, and
thankfully not much has
changed, making it a true
New York institution.

GREENBLATT'S

*8017 Sunset Boulevard,
Los Angeles, CA 90046*

Opened on the east end
of the Sunset strip in
1926, predating many of
the now-famous clubs
and bars surrounding it,
this deli is still managed
by only its second owner
since the 1940s—and feels
like a throwback to
that era.

KATZ'S DELICATESSEN

*205 E Houston Street,
New York, NY 10002*

Perhaps the quintessential American deli, dating back to 1888, Katz's smokes their meats for more than thirty days to ensure a blissful eating experience.

LANGER'S

*704 S Alvarado Street,
Los Angeles, CA 90057*

In its downtown location since 1945, some say it serves the best pastrami in the world. Try their #19 sandwich, its most popular, with hot pastrami, coleslaw, russian dressing, and a slice of swiss cheese on baked rye bread, and try debating its status as king.

SARGE'S DELI

*548 Third Avenue,
New York, NY 10016*

It's been open since 1954 and is perhaps best known as the place that'll deliver to all of Manhattan 365 days a year. It was founded by a cop named Katz and is still family run. It might not win accolades for its quality, but it's certainly reliable.

CANTER'S

*419 N Fairfax Avenue,
Los Angeles, CA 90036*

Featured in countless TV shows and movies, it's perhaps the quintessential Los Angeles deli, as it's a twenty-four-hour establishment with a super cool, super big art deco sign. It's now known more for its late-night crowd than for the quality of its food.

EISENBERG'S SANDWICH SHOP

174 Fifth Avenue,
New York, NY 10010

Somewhere between a deli, a diner, and a sandwich shop, this tiny Fifth Avenue hole-in-the-wall (really a glorified counter) has been around since 1929 and has been passed down by its owner to a regular customer (as its new owner) a few times over the years.

FACTOR'S DELI

9420 Pico Boulevard,
Los Angeles, CA 90035

With a convenient location midway between Hollywood and Santa Monica, this business on Pico has been attracting loyal customers since its opening in 1969.

RUSS & DAUGHTERS CAFE

127 Orchard Street,
New York, NY 10002

On the appetizing store's 100th anniversary, the fourth-generation children of its founders opened a new cafe next door, breathing new life into the deli scene and becoming the paramount example of the new wave of hip delis popping up around town.

FREEDMAN'S

2619 Sunset Boulevard,
Los Angeles, CA 90026

Canadian-reared siblings created this iconoclast, irreverent take on the classic Jewish eatery in hip Silver Lake.

CHINESE FOOD

New Yorkers will argue ad nauseam about their Chinese food; they say there's nothing like it. And it's true: the food in Chinatown and Queens has its own particular flavor, history, and iconic status in the cultural fabric of New York. But Los Angeles has its own unique history, style, and brand of Chinese food, one that's just as complex and delicious, the heart and soul of which can be found in the San Gabriel Valley.

The Chinese population grew rapidly in the Lower East Side of Manhattan in the 1870s, when many business owners began to cater to the tastes of Anglo Americans, combining flavors from the East with simplified recipes that would appeal to Western customers. In 1915, a loophole opened that allowed Chinese merchants to obtain visas as restaurant owners, bringing many more Chinese cooks to New York over the following decades. The distinct effort to cater to American tastes continued, amending the cooking styles and flavors of China for an American palate. Hence, dishes like lo mein and chop suey were born—and proliferated in New York.

By the 1970s and into the 1980s, immigrants from Taiwan and Hong Kong flocked back to California, but this time down to the San Gabriel Valley on the northeast corner of Los Angeles. By the 1980s, the San Gabriel Valley started to be known as the first suburban Chinatown.

While Chinese food continued to refine and develop its own particular style in New York—with Shun Lee Palace becoming the first Chinese restaurant to receive a four-star review from the *New York Times* in 1967, for example—the food in SGV remained more loyal to its roots. It's there that Chinese chefs could cook authentic dishes from their home for an upper-middle class of Chinese clientele.

New York and Los Angeles have drastically different histories and vibes and types of restaurants when it comes to Chinese food, so perhaps it doesn't matter which is "better"... you can eat extraordinarily well in both places.

REDFARM

*2170 Broadway,
New York, NY 10024*

*529 Hudson Street,
New York, NY 10014*

A modern classic from
Ed Schoenfeld and
Joe Ng, it's famous for
its Pac-Man dumplings
and elevated classics.

NORTHERN CAFE

Multiple Locations

An SGV original, famous
for its beef rolls, dump-
lings, and dan dan
noodles, opened a fresh
new location in Westwood
(near UCLA) in 2016 and
another in Beverly Grove
in 2017, spreading its
delicious food to a
wider audience.

WO HOP

*17 Mott Street,
New York, NY 10013*

Chinatown's second-oldest
restaurant and simply
a classic of Chinese
American fare.

TASTY NOODLE HOUSE

*8054 W Third Street,
Los Angeles, CA 90048*

Sometimes simple can be
supreme, as with this joint
that serves some of the
best noodles in the nation.

SZECHUAN HOUSE

*133-47 Roosevelt Avenue,
Flushing, NY 11354*

Some say it's the best
Szechuan cuisine in
the country!

CHENGDU TASTE

*3233, 828 W Valley Boulevard,
Alhambra, CA 91803*

The crown jewel of
Szechuan cuisine in
the SGV.

NOM WAH

13 Doyers Street,
New York, NY 10013

Dating back to the 1920s, this original Chinatown staple still charms customers out of its original location but has also modernized and added an additional location in Nolita.

SICHUAN IMPRESSION

1900 W Valley Boulevard,
Alhambra, CA 91803

Though less lauded than Chengdu Taste, this restaurant features specialties from the same region that are just as tasty—and may seem just as unique to your average Chinese food–eating American.

JOE'S SHANGHAI

136-21 Thirty-Seventh Avenue,
Flushing, NY 11354

Chef Kiu Sang "Joe" Si opened his eponymous restaurant in 1995 in Flushing and quickly became famous for his delectable soup dumplings.

DIN TAI FUNG

1108 S Baldwin Avenue,
Arcadia, CA 91007

The Southern California king of soup dumplings.

DUMPLING GALAXY

42-35 Main Street,
Flushing, NY 11355

The dumpling house is famous for its many innovative varieties.

MEIZHOU DONGPO RESTAURANT

10250 Santa Monica Boulevard,
Los Angeles, CA 90067

One of the few Jonathan Gold–approved Chinese restaurants outside of the SGV.

FAST FOOD

New Yorkers love to walk, and fast. With more than eight million people constantly on the move, the city has spawned a series of food options as hurried as the residents. Halal, hot dog, toasted nut, and pretzel carts are all products—and symbols—of a fast-paced walking culture.

Angelenos love to drive. Well, if they don't exactly love it, they all still do it. With an estimated 6.5 million cars, Los Angeles has spawned a series of food options ready to pick up and eat while driving.

> "BY COMPARISON WITH OTHER LESS HECTIC DAYS, THE CITY IS UNCOMFORTABLE AND INCONVENIENT; BUT NEW YORKERS TEMPERAMENTALLY DO NOT CRAVE COMFORT AND CONVENIENCE—IF THEY DID THEY WOULD LIVE ELSEWHERE."

—E.B. White

LA's restaurants and food needed to be *fast*. In 1948, the first In-N-Out burger opened in Baldwin Park, California, with its own two-way intercom system, making it an early pioneer of the drive-through (building on earlier renditions introduced in Texas and Missouri). McDonald's opened that same year in close-by San Bernardino with its incredibly fast window service.

Here's how the two cities' fast-food joints stack up.

STREET PRETZELS

Multiple locations

German and Dutch immigrants brought pretzels to Pennsylvania as early as the late-eighteenth century, then the snack made its way up to New York to feed industrial workers in the mid-nineteenth century and have persisted to this day.

MISTER SOFTEE

Multiple locations

Although the omnipresent soft-serve ice cream truck debuted in Philadelphia in 1956, it can now be found in any neighborhood at any time of the year and represents an iconic New York dessert.

HARLEM'S BLUE SKY DELI (HAJJI'S)

2135 First Avenue, New York, NY 10029

Some call it magical. Some just call it delicious. The Chop Cheese. It's a bodega specialty made famous throughout the mom-and-pop shops in Harlem and the Bronx and perfected at Harlem's Blue Sky Deli, which is actually better known locally as Hajji's. The sandwich is a delicious mix of beef, onions, and American cheese on a hero roll (sort of like Philly's cheesesteak).

FOOD TRUCKS

Multiple locations

Before high-end chefs started retrofitting vans, cooks across LA were selling all types of food from inconspicuous trucks that provided a quick-and-easy anytime meal for residents across the city.

FOSTERS FREEZE

Multiple locations

George Foster founded his fast-food shop in Inglewood in 1946, boasting amazing soft-serve ice cream and milkshakes and resulting in the current slogan of "California's Original Soft-Serve." Its original location still proudly stands, but it also has more than one hundred locations across the state.

THE HAT

5505 Rosemead Boulevard, Temple City, CA 91780

Serving its quick and easy pastrami to walk-up customers since 1951 in the San Gabriel Valley.

DELICIOSO COCO HELADO

Multiple locations

Alfredo Thiebaud began selling the quintessential Latin American and the Caribbean tropical treat out of paper cups in the late 1960s from a pushcart in the hardscrabble area of the South Bronx, eventually building his business—and himself—into a local icon up until his untimely death in 2014. Still, the carts remain family owned and operated and extremely popular (and delicious) across the Bronx.

NUTS 4 NUTS

Multiple locations

Argentinian Alejandro Rad started as a pushcart vendor in Manhattan in the late 1980s, and by 1993 he launched his own brand of honey-roasted nuts inspired by the French-Argentinian staple. He now has more than one hundred carts across the City.

SHAKE SHACK

Madison Avenue & E Twenty-Third Street, New York, NY 10010

(Original location)

Famed restaurateur Danny Meyer launched Shake Shack in Madison Square Park in 2004 in what was intended to be a single location. The burger joint exploded in popularity, and Meyer quickly expanded, growing the franchise to more than 180 locations across the planet and boasting a per-location profit higher than McDonald's.

RANDY'S DONUTS

805 W Manchester Boulevard, Inglewood, CA 90301

The original Inglewood bakery boasts a massive thirty-five-foot donut sculpture on its roof, which it wears proudly like the crown it deserves.

ASTRO BURGER

5601 Melrose Avenue, Los Angeles, CA 90038

Across from the Paramount studio lot, this counter shack started as a typical hamburger joint in 1975 but now has a relatively expansive menu, including many Greek specialty items.

IN-N-OUT

13766 Francisquito Avenue, Baldwin Park, CA 91706

(Original location)

With humble beginnings as a drive-through-only hamburger stand in the Baldwin Park neighborhood of California, it has year after year maintained impeccable quality and steady growth across the southwest US, making its current president and majority owner Lynsi Snyder, granddaughter of its founder, the youngest female billionaire in the US. Ask for your burger "Animal Style" for grilled onions and extra secret sauce. You won't be disappointed.

HALAL GUYS

Multiple locations

Started by three Egyptian American immigrants in 1990 as a hot-dog cart on Fifty-Third and Sixth Avenue, the partners shifted to cooking authentic Islamic cuisine to satisfy the untapped demand fueled by the city's thousands of cab drivers. That's how the now-famous platter of chicken and gyro over rice was born, transforming the cart into an internationally franchised brand.

PAPAYA KING

Multiple locations

In 1932, a creative Greek immigrant named Gus Poulos vacationed in Cuba and came back inspired to launch the city's first juice bar. He eventually started serving hot dogs out of the same shop, and thus the unusual combination of tropical juices and hot dogs was born. In the 1970s, he dipped his toe into franchising, allowing entrepreneur Nicholas Gray to open a Papaya King on his own; however, just a few years later, Gray closed shop, then reopened as Gray's Papaya. Gray's expanded like wildfire across the city, perhaps eclipsing Papaya King in popularity. Grab a dog at either place—still a hot dog, but way better than a dirty water dog from a street cart!

ZANKOU CHICKEN

805 W Manchester Boulevard, Inglewood, CA 90301

Armenian entrepreneur Mardiros Iskenderian founded his first chicken spot in 1983 when his family immigrated to Los Angeles from Lebanon, serving spit-roasted chicken with a family recipe of super thick garlic spread. It has since expanded to eight locations and become a true city icon, serving the expansive Armenian American population and beyond.

PINK'S HOT DOGS

Multiple locations

Paul and Betty Pink started selling hot dogs out of a pushcart in 1939 on the corner of La Brea and Melrose near the Paramount lot in the center of the city, eventually purchasing the land on which they stood in 1946 and erecting a modest hut of sorts. The business stayed solid over the years, attracting locals, including many movie stars (the walls of the hut are plastered with more than two hundred signed photos of celebrity customers!) and was passed down to Paul and Betty's children in the mid-1980s.

BREAKFAST, BRUNCH, BAGELS & BAKERIES

New York has been known as the city that never sleeps, and perhaps that's why it's also a city with no time for breakfast. While New Yorkers are constantly on the go, Los Angeles seems to be the only place where coffee shops and brunch spots overflow with people on a Tuesday at 11:00 a.m. (Does anybody work in this city?)

> ## "THE BAGEL, AN UNSWEETENED DOUGHNUT WITH RIGOR MORTIS."

—Beatrice and Ira Freeman, the *New York Times*

So which city does it better? Sure, New York has bagels, but Los Angeles has breakfast burritos. And when it comes to breakfast—and coffee, bakeries, pastries, bagels, eggs, and so on—you'll find plenty of excellent options across the board in both coasts.

> ## "IF IT WEREN'T FOR THE COFFEE, I'D HAVE NO IDENTIFIABLE PERSONALITY WHATSOEVER."

—David Letterman

NORMA'S

*119 W Fifty-Sixth Street,
New York, NY 10019*

What's more New York than a $1,000 plate of eggs? Nothing. Check out this over-the-top Midtown institution for a delicious meal—or just to ogle at the outlandish menu!

SQIRL

*720 N Virgil Avenue #4,
Los Angeles, CA 90029*

Jessica Koslow's tiny East Hollywood preserves shop took the culinary world by storm in 2011, inventing and popularizing a new style of California cuisine that's fresh, local, and incredibly delicious. The style now defines the city. You may wait hours for one of the few seats in her adorably tiny shop, but it's a meal you'll not soon forget.

CITY BAKERY

*3 W Eighteenth Street,
New York, NY 10011*

Maury Rubin opened City Bakery in 1990 after falling in love with baking and taking a pastry course in France. Since then, the City Bakery has endured with its rich pastries and überthick hot chocolate, hosting a popular "hot chocolate festival" for more than twenty-five years.

JOAN'S ON THIRD

*8350 W Third Street,
Los Angeles, CA 90048*

Joan McNamara founded her eponymous counter-service restaurant in 1995 when the stretch of Third Street between Beverly Hills and Mid-Century had little going on, but her delicious food and impeccable interior design style has made it a Hollywood hot spot for more than twenty years.

DONUT PUB

*203 W Fourteenth Street,
New York, NY 10011*

This 24/7 counter-only spot on West Fourteenth assaults the senses with an indelible sugar rush upon entering. It's been serving its freshly made donuts since 1964.

INTELLIGENTSIA

*3922 Sunset Boulevard,
Los Angeles, CA 90029*

This third-wave coffee pioneer founded by Doug Zell and Emily Mange opened its first shop outside of Chicago in 2007 in trendy Silver Lake, helping to define that area as a cultural and culinary heavyweight.

SULLIVAN STREET BAKERY

*236 Ninth Avenue,
New York, NY 10011*

Jim Lahey opened his bakery in 1994, seeking to create a loaf like those he loved in Europe and has grown his little shop into a veritable empire, providing countless restaurants around town with his freshly baked bread daily.

LA BREA BAKERY

*468 South La Brea Avenue,
Los Angeles, CA 90036*

Pioneering chef Nancy Silverton's bread-baking mecca opened in Los Angeles in 1989 and has been supplying the world with otherworldly bread ever since.

ESS-A-BAGEL

*831 Third Avenue,
New York, NY 10022*

These oversize, impossibly soft and plump bagels have been dominating the scene since this shop opened in 1976.

LA MASCOTA

*2715 Whittier Boulevard,
Los Angeles, CA 90023*

An eastside cornerstone for more than sixty years, serving some of the city's best Mexican pastries, including amazing pan dolce and tamales.

VENIERO'S

*342 E Eleventh Street,
New York, NY 10003*

This Italian pastry shop, famous for its cakes and cannoli, has been a downtown fixture since 1894.

PORTO'S BAKERY

*2913, 3614 W Magnolia
Boulevard,
Burbank, CA 91505*

Cuban immigrant Rosa Porto opened her first bakery in Los Angeles in 1976. More than forty years later, the business is still family owned and operated, selling its famous (and trademarked) Potato Ball to nearly five million customers annually across four Southern California locations.

VESELKA

144 Second Avenue,
New York, NY 10003

With beginnings as a Ukrainian restaurant, this downtown institution now serves up classic eggs dishes (in a more standard Classic American Diner fashion) side by side with pierogi and blintz (keeping its tradition alive).

JOHN O'GROATS

10516 Pico Boulevard,
Los Angeles, CA 90064

Serving only breakfast and lunch since 1982, this family-owned restaurant has found lasting success with its fluffy biscuits and signature Huevos O'Groats, among other delicious breakfast staples.

DOMINIQUE ANSEL

189 Spring Street,
New York, NY 10012

This outstanding bakery is home to the famed Cronut—an insanely delicious cross between a croissant and a donut—and still has a long line every morning after the trademarked Frankenpastry set the world on fire.

DU-PAR'S

6333 W Third Street,
Los Angeles, CA 90036

Opened in 1938 at the original farmers market on Third & Fairfax, this diner has thrived there ever since, serving breakfast staples (including its incredibly fluffy pancakes, frequently voted among the best in the nation).

SUSHI

In LA, it's all about the strip-mall hidden gem. In NY, it's all about the exclusive and expensive.

Although the facts have been hotly debated, most sources say sushi first made its American debut at Kawafuku Restaurant in Los Angeles's Little Tokyo in the early 1960s.

> "LA, IT'S NICE, BUT I THINK OF SUNSHINE AND PEOPLE ON ROLLERBLADES EATING SUSHI. NEW YORK, I THINK OF NIGHTTIME, I THINK OF TIMES SQUARE AND BROADWAY AND NIGHTLIFE AND THE CITY THAT NEVER SLEEPS."
>
> —Jimmy Fallon

Fast-forward to today and you'll find exceptional raw fish joints on both coasts. Chefs Eddie Huang and Michael Voltaggio summed it up best in a 2016 *Hollywood Reporter* interview, with Huang saying "L.A. definitely is on top. If you want cheap sushi, you can get really cheap, high-quality sushi in L.A. In New York it's like $200 and up. If you're not paying $200, don't eat it, you know?" Voltaggio chimed in as well, "[I] experience[d] a four-star *New York Times* sushi restaurant. It was amazing. But we have that level of sushi for half that price here [in LA]."

It's true: New York has some outstanding high-end places, but you'll have to pay the big bucks. In Los Angeles, some of the prime spots can be found in dingy strip malls or even the back of a hamburger joint!

NEW YORK

LOS ANGELES

SUSHI YASUDA

*204 E Forty-Third Street,
New York, NY 10017*

Serving consistent quality since 1999, this Midtown restaurant dons a Michelin star and classically refined atmosphere to match its steep prices.

SUSHI PARK

*8539 Sunset Boulevard #20,
West Hollywood, CA 90069*

This barren hole-in-the-wall serves some of the city's best fish on the second floor of a strip mall on the Sunset Strip. What it lacks in decor it makes up for in celebrity sightings.

SUSHI OF GARI

*402 E Seventy-Eighth Street,
New York, NY 10075*

The godfather of pre-saucing sushi for his customers, rather than letting them over soak it in soy sauce, Masatoshi "Gari" Sugio has been pioneering sushi in Manhattan since he opened his own spot on the Upper East Side in 1997.

KING'S BURGERS (GOT SUSHI?)

*9345 Reseda Boulevard,
Northridge, CA 91324*

Locals know about this outstanding sushi bar hidden in the back of an unassuming burger joint— something you'd only find in LA.

MASA

*10 Columbus Circle,
New York, NY 10019*

A once-in-a-lifetime kind of place, this three–Michelin star temple will run you nearly a grand per person, but critics seem to agree that chef Masa Takayama's restaurant is a classic. Either way, it surely epitomizes the sky-high prices of New York.

SUSHI TIME

*8103 Beverly Boulevard,
Los Angeles, CA 90048*

This midcity gem epitomizes the Los Angeles strip-mall vibe with delicious fish, cheap prices, and frequent low-key celebrity sightings.

SUSHI NAKAZAWA

*23 Commerce Street,
New York, NY 10014*

A protégé of Jiro, from Netflix documentary *Jiro Dreams of Sushi* fame, Daisuke Nakazawa serves up delectable omakase at this West Village spot in a hip yet comfortable setting with out-of-this-world service.

SUSHI GEN

*422 E Second Street,
Los Angeles, CA 90012*

A downtown institution with long lines and no frills, serving fresh omakase since 1980.

SUSHI GINZA ONODERA

461 Fifth Avenue,
New York, NY 10017

An offshoot of a revered Tokyo restaurant that'll run you upward of $400 a person. Is it worth it? Yeah, probably.

GO'S MART

22330 Sherman Way C12,
Canoga Park, CA 91303

It's not the simple green block-letter sign that only says "SUSHI" nor the blinding orange-colored walls that make this strip-mall gem way out in the boonies worth the trip.

> ## "MAKING SUSHI IS AN ART, AND EXPERIENCE IS EVERYTHING."

—Nobu Matsuhisa

FOOD HALLS, FARMERS MARKETS, FAIRS & GROCERIES

Public markets have defined cities, their culture, and values since the shift to agrarian culture thousands of years ago. What better way to understand and explore a city than within the walls and between the stalls of a city's food markets?

> "WHEN I'M IN LOS ANGELES, MY WIFE AND I GO TO THE FARMERS MARKET WITH THE KIDS EVERY SUNDAY."
>
> —Wolfgang Puck

CHELSEA MARKET

75 Ninth Avenue, New York, NY 10011

Built in the former Nabisco factory near the Hudson River and High Line—the same factory where the Oreo was invented!—this massive food hall occupies the entire block between Fifteenth and Sixteenth Streets and Ninth and Tenth Avenues. Nabisco left the site in the 1950s, and it laid dormant and quite dangerous until 1997, when a developer bought the property and transformed it into the culinary and shopping destination it is today. Fun fact: In 2018, Google bought the property for more than $2 billion!

GRAND CENTRAL TERMINAL

89 E Forty-Second Street, New York, NY 10017

Not only is it an architectural masterpiece and landmark, GCT also features an exciting mashup of highbrow and common fare. It's got everything from the Oyster Bar & Restaurant, serving bougie seafood since 1913, to the Campbell, a stunning 1920s-style speakeasy, to the Michelin-starred Agern, an Icelandic fine restaurant, to stalls from Shake Shack, Magnolia Bakery, Chirping Chicken, and a market with fresh produce and baked goods by Zabar.

LA'S FARMERS MARKET

6333 W Third Street, Los Angeles, CA 90036

In 1934, two entrepreneurs approached the owner of a large oil field at Third and Fairfax with "an idea," which was to create a central hub where farmers could sell their goods. Less than a year later, the operation was so successful that farmers started taking up permanent residence at the site. In 1948, the famous clock tower went up with "An Idea" inscribed on its side, and ever since then, the farmers market has been an iconic and useful hub for residents and tourists alike. Its popularity only increased when the Grove shopping center went up next door.

GRAND CENTRAL MARKET

317 S Broadway, Los Angeles, CA 90013

This landmark originally opened as a place to grocery shop in the bustling downtown LA in 1917, but it ebbed and flowed over time as the neighborhood changed. After a particularly low point in the 2008 recession, owner Adele Yellin stepped up with a vision to bring in cutting-edge chefs and foodie entrepreneurs, attracting the likes of Eggslut, Wexler's, and Horse Thief BBQ, who sit alongside legacy vendors like the famed Mexican spice shop Chiles Secos.

SMORGASBURG

90 Kent Avenue, Brooklyn, NY 11211

Launched in 2011 in an empty parking lot in Williamsburg along the East River, this food market has quickly grown into the largest weekly open-air food market in the country. It's also established itself as an incubator for up-and-coming food trendsetters and as a culinary institution in its own right.

EATALY

200 Fifth Avenue, New York, NY 10010

Italian entrepreneur Oscar Farinetti opened the first Eataly in Turin in 2007, combining the best aspects of a farmers market, grocery store, food stall, and everything Italian cooking into one megastore. In 2010, the first US location opened across from Madison Square Park in a 50,000-square-foot facility to much fanfare and acclaim. It's a shrine to all things Italia.

QUEENS NIGHT MARKET

New York Hall of Science, Flushing Meadows Corona Park,

Corona, NY 11368

Founder John Wang intended the open-air night market to represent every culture and country that composes New York, so an evening spent here can be among the most surprising, colorful, and eclectic experiences the city has to offer.

SMORGASBURG LA

777 Alameda Street, Los Angeles, CA 90021

Launched five years after the original Williamsburg location, the downtown LA outpost has quickly become the largest outdoor food market in the city, featuring more than ninety vendors every Sunday.

EATALY

10250 Santa Monica Boulevard, Los Angeles, CA 90067

Following expansion of the Eataly concept in New York, Tokyo, Boston, Chicago, and elsewhere, it finally opened in Los Angeles in 2017, occupying a cornerstone space in the newly remodeled Westfield Shopping Center in Century City. It's the largest Eataly in the world.

626 NIGHT MARKET

285 W Huntington Drive, Arcadia, CA 91007

Named for the San Gabriel Valley's area code, this monthly affair has claimed to be the original and largest Asian food market—and with more than 250 vendors, it's almost more of a festival than a market. Be sure to come hungry.

URBANSPACE @ VANDERBILT

East Forty-Fifth & Vanderbilt Avenue, New York, NY 10169

Popping up across the street from Grand Central Terminal, this permanent indoor food market features mini outposts of some of the city's best restaurants, including Roberta's, Ippudo, Dough, and more. Urbanspace itself began in the UK in the 1970s, jumping over the pond in 1993 to kick-start some of the city's best markets, including the Union Square Holiday Market and Madison Square Eats.

ZABAR'S

2245 Broadway, New York, NY 10024

Jewish immigrants Louis and Lillian Zabar founded this appetizing shop in 1934 on the Upper West Side, serving high-quality foods at fair prices. It has become a true New York institution for grocery shopping, catering, and deli and appetizing foods, and it remains in the Zabar family to this day.

UNION SQUARE GREENMARKET

E Seventeenth Street & Union Square W, New York, NY 10003

Featuring local producers of fruits, vegetables, meats, dairy, flowers, and other amazing goods, the crown jewel of the city's farmers markets has been open for more than forty years and serves more than 250,000 people over the course of Monday, Wednesday, Friday, and Saturday each week.

CORPORATION FOOD HALL

724 S Spring Street, Los Angeles, CA 90014

Though quite small, this collection of top-tier culinary outposts, including Gyoza Boyza, South City Fried Chicken, and Funculo, proves the whole's greater than the sum of its parts and is worth a visit to downtown LA.

BAY CITIES ITALIAN DELI & MARKET

1517 Lincoln Boulevard, Santa Monica, CA 90401

The humble Italian market sells the city's best sandwich— the revered Godmother, which features Genoa salami, prosciutto, mortadella, coppacola, ham, and provolone on one of the best bread rolls on the planet—and has been serving local customers since the 1920s.

HOLLYWOOD FARMERS' MARKET

Hollywood Boulevard & Sunset Boulevard, Los Angeles, CA 90028

This standby features fresh California produce, local culinary vendors, and street musicians in the heart of Hollywood every Saturday since 1991.

JAPAN VILLAGE

934 Third Avenue, Brooklyn, NY 11232

This massive all-things-Japanese market, grocery, and food-stall hub opened in 2018 in Brooklyn's Industry City, promising to bring an Eataly-style brouhaha to Japanese cuisine in the borough.

LITTLE TOKYO

335 East Second Street, Los Angeles, CA 90012

This is the largest official Japan town in the nation, and while it's not a food or farmers market, the downtown area has an extensive assortment of authentic restaurants and an outdoor mall. It's also the birthplace of the california roll and the site of one of the oldest operating food establishments in the city (a Japanese candy store called Fugetsu-Do Bakery Shop), so it's well worth a visit.

THE STEAK HOUSE & THE VEGAN

The modern-day steak house is a true New York original. Some of the earliest New York restaurants, including the still standing Fraunces Tavern (established in the 1760s) and the nearby Delmonico's (established in the 1830s) would have served beef, and the proper steak houses as we know them today arrived with the Old Homestead Steakhouse in 1868, and Keen's and Peter Luger's shortly thereafter.

Los Angeles has its fair share of top-tier steak houses, but it's really a champion of establishments on the polar opposite end of the spectrum.

Ever since the 1960s, when an eventual cult leader opened his infamous raw and vegan restaurant, the Source, on the Sunset Strip, Los Angeles has been an innovator in plant-based dining.

Perhaps nothing explains the dichotomy better than a classic *Sex & the City* episode (Season 3, Episode 14, "Sex and Another City") where the gang heads to Los Angeles for a week. Once there, Miranda catches up with an old friend at a steak house in LA only to find that he spits out his meat after a few bites to stay thin and impress his bosses.

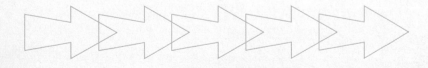

PETER LUGER

*178 Broadway,
Brooklyn, NY 11211*

Carl Luger opened his eponymous "cafe, billiards, and bowling alley" in 1887 in Williamsburg more than a decade before the Williamsburg Bridge was built. In 1950, following Luger's death, a local businessman named Sol Forman bought the restaurant at auction, helping propel it to its iconic status as a Michelin-starred "American Classic" by the James Beard Foundation.

CAFE GRATITUDE

*639 N Larchmont Boulevard,
Los Angeles, CA 90004*

A Los Angeles vegan institution since its inception in 2004, this plant-based restaurant serves dishes with names like "Glorious," "Humble," and "Evolved," operating under "Sacred Commerce." Its owners describe that concept by saying "we provide inspired service, honest and transparent communication, and express gratitude for the richness of our lives."

PORTER HOUSE

*10 Columbus Circle,
New York, NY 10019*

Celebrity chef Michael Lomonaco's upscale steak house has topped many "best of" lists since its opening in the chic Time Warner Center in 2006.

CROSSROADS KITCHEN

*8284 Melrose Avenue,
Los Angeles, CA 90046*

The brick-and-mortar post for celebrity chef Tal Ronnen, who famously crafted Oprah's cleanse diet and catered Ellen's wedding.

4 CHARLES PRIME RIB

3004, 4 Charles Street,
New York, NY 10014

Intimate, cavernous, refined steak house with an insanely good burger from revered Chicago chef Brendan Sodikoff.

GRACIAS MADRE

8905 Melrose Avenue,
West Hollywood, CA 90069

Plant-based Mexican cuisine in chic West Hollywood that's as hip as it is cruelty free.

KEENS

72 W Thirty-Sixth Street,
New York, NY 10018

A staple since 1885, this steak house famously served the top actors at the center of the Herald Square theater district during the turn of the century and is still booming today.

REAL FOOD DAILY

414 N La Cienega Boulevard,
Los Angeles, CA 90048

An original vegan destination, it has been innovating in plant-based cuisine since its opening in 1993.

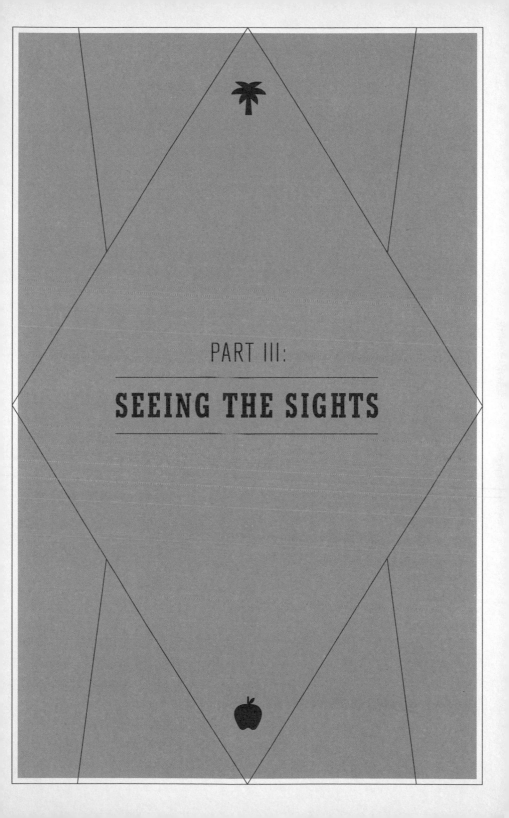

PART III:

SEEING THE SIGHTS

MUSEUMS

Despite being ridiculed for decades as a black hole for true culture (beyond the movies, of course), Los Angeles has its fair share of world-class art—and has, in fact, long been a beacon for artists. Did you know Andy Warhol's first gallery show was held in Beverly Hills? The tradition remains alive and well, especially with the 2015 opening of the Broad—and its selfie-inducing contemporary art.

To competently guide a New Yorker through Los Angeles's art scene—and vice versa—takes more than a consideration of the type of art featured within an institution's walls. Sure, there's MOCA in downtown LA, with its contemporary collection, and MoMA in Manhattan, with its world-class modern art. But you must take into account the entire experience of visiting the place—the neighborhood, the architecture, how you'll spend the rest of your day—to understand and appreciate either.

Take, for instance, the new Whitney Museum in Manhattan. It's a glorious triumph of architecture by Renzo Piano, perched on the waterfront in one of New York's trendiest neighborhoods. Compare that with the Getty Villa: a miraculously restored mansion nestled into the cliffs overlooking the sea in Malibu. One houses American art and the other showcases treasures from antiquity, yet the experience of visiting either somehow feels more similar than different.

INSTAGRAM SPOTS

It's said a picture is worth a thousand words—and on Instagram, a good travel pic might be worth a thousand likes. Beyond the Statue of Liberty or the Santa Monica Pier, where can you go to get the best posts?

NEW YORK

LOS ANGELES

I FEEL YOU BABY

What:

Iconic black bubble-letter script on a large white wall by mural artist @baronvonfancy and commissioned by #TheNewAllen.

Where:

Outside of Baby Brasa (173 Seventh Avenue South, New York, NY, 10014), chef and model Franco Noriega's Peruvian restaurant

PINK WALL

What:

The outer walls of the Paul Smith flagship store are covered in a pitch-perfect millennial pink.

Where:

The west-facing wall of the Paul Smith flagship store in WeHo (8221 Melrose Avenue, Los Angeles, CA 90046)

BOWERY GRAFFITI WALL

What:

Massive wall in the Lower East Side featuring a rotating cast of artists. Originally tagged by Keith Haring, the wall is now overseen by Goldman Global Arts and features a revolving door of premiere street artists.

Where:

Corner of Houston & Bowery
(76 E Houston Street, New York, NY 10012)

VENICE BEACH ART WALLS

What:

Originally part of the Venice Pavilion built in the 1960s, these walls quickly became a hotbed of illegal graffiti. Yet when the pavilion was torn down in 1999, a portion remained intact, and graffiti became legalized on these historic structures.

Where:

Venice Beach Boardwalk
(800 Ocean Front Walk, Venice, CA 90291)

FLATIRON BUILDING

What:

The iconic wedge-shaped landmark fit snugly into the corner where Fifth Avenue and Broadway intersect.

Where:

175 Fifth Avenue, New York, NY 10010

URBAN LIGHTS

What:

LACMA's permanent lamppost installation by artist Chris Burden.

Where:

5905 Wilshire Boulevard, Los Angeles, CA 90036

MONICA'S APARTMENT FROM *FRIENDS*

What:

While the TV show was shot in Los Angeles, the exterior of Monica, Rachel, Joey, and Chandler's building does exist in New York.

Where:

90 Bedford Street, at the corner of Grove Street in Greenwich Village

WORKING REPLICA OF CENTRAL PERK

What:

You can see the real couch from Central Perk and a working replica of the cafe.

Where:

On the Warner Brothers Studio tour

THE DINER FROM *SEINFELD*

What:

The exterior of the famous diner from Seinfeld is Tom's Restaurant, but the TV cropped out the name "Tom" from the shot.

Where:

2880 Broadway (on the corner of West 112th Street)

CIRCUS LIQUOR FROM *CLUELESS*

What:

The iconic spot where Cher ditches her boyfriend and gets mugged somewhere deep in the Valley, then gets stranded without a car.

Where:

5600 Vineland Ave, North Hollywood, CA 91601

NYC: WHITNEY MUSEUM OF AMERICAN ART

99 Gansevoort Street, New York, NY 10014

Designed by Pritzker Prize–winning architect Renzo Piano, the Whitney Museum's 2015 building looms over the Hudson River in the ever-hip Meatpacking neighborhood, providing breathtaking views of Manhattan, the Statue of Liberty, and New Jersey. Heiress, philanthropist, and artist Gertrude Vanderbilt Whitney offered her impressive collection to the Metropolitan Museum of Art in 1929, but the Met declined, stating it did not show American artworks. That sparked Whitney to establish her own museum dedicated to American art. The collection now features gems spanning the entire history of American art.

Spend a day by the water, enjoying fantastic views in a museum whose building might be the best piece in the collection.

LA: THE GETTY VILLA

17985 Pacific Coast Highway, Pacific Palisades CA 90272

Oil baron and billionaire John Paul Getty first opened a small gallery adjacent his Malibu mansion in 1954 to showcase his massive collection of Greek and Roman antiquity, but he soon outgrew the space. He set out to construct a veritable palace in its place, modeled after the Villa of the Papyri in the ancient Roman town of Herculaneum. It premiered in 1974, though Getty never set foot in the Villa himself, having died two years earlier. Technically located in the Pacific Palisades neighborhood of Los Angeles, the center is perched on the bluffs directly on the border of Malibu. It closed from 1997 to 2006 for renovations, and is now a stunning, can't-miss destination.

NYC: AMERICAN MUSEUM OF NATURAL HISTORY

Central Park West & Seventy-Ninith Street, New York, NY 10024

One of the largest museums in the world, the AMNH houses more than thirty million specimens and features exhibits that span all of Earth's history and that of outer space. The fourth floor houses the expansive dinosaur exhibits, which feature fossils of the Tyrannosaurus rex, among other famous dinos, while the museum's entrance on Central Park West, officially known as the Theodore Roosevelt Rotunda, features the famous Allosaurus and Barosaurus display.

Premiere natural history collections that are great for kids.

LA: LA BREA TAR PITS

5801 Wilshire Boulevard, Los Angeles, CA 90036

While the fossils on display at the La Brea Tar Pits date only as far back at 50,000 years—65 million years after the dinosaur bones featured at the NY Natural History Museum—the museum's collection is no less iconic for the city in which it's displayed. In fact, part of Los Angeles's own natural history museum "family" (the main site located at Exposition Park at 900 W Exposition Boulevard), the Tar Pits feature incredible examples of Ice Age animals, from the mastodon to the saber-toothed cat, which were discovered on its very location, and thus provide hours of fun and "living history" education for families.

NYC: METROPOLITAN MUSEUM OF ART

1000 Fifth Avenue, New York, NY 10028

The largest museum in the United States and the third-most-visited museum in the world, the Met features works of art and historical objects from across a vast array of time periods, cultures, and regions, all of which are displayed in its two-million-square-foot building on Fifth Avenue that opened in 1880.

Iconic and massive institutions.

LA: LOS ANGELES COUNTY MUSEUM OF ART

5905 Wilshire Boulevard, Los Angeles, CA 90036

While LACMA only boasts an annual visitor count of 1.5 million to the Met's 7 million, it remains the largest museum in the western United States.

Conceived in 1965, the museum's collections contain objects from across cultures, continents, and time periods. The museum sits on Miracle Mile in Mid-City on Wilshire Boulevard, and ever since 2008, Chris Burden's "Urban Lights," an art installation of 202 old city streetlamps arranged in a geometric pattern, has graced its front lawn, adding to the museum's iconic landmark status.

NYC: NATIONAL MUSEUM OF MATHEMATICS

11 East Twenty-Sixth Street, New York, NY 10010

New York City's only museum dedicated to mathematics, MoMath, as it's commonly called, opened in 2012 and features hands-on exhibits illustrating scientific and mathematical concepts to its thousands of yearly visitors.

Educational, hands-on science and math centers.

LA: CALIFORNIA SCIENCE CENTER

700 Exposition Park Drive, Los Angeles, CA 90037

Jam-packed with hands-on exhibitions and learning experiences on the natural world, science, and technology, the California Science Center has been delighting and educating children since its opening in 1998. It also houses the decommissioned space shuttle *Endeavour*, which is remarkable to see in person, whether as a child or adult.

NYC: INTREPID SEA, AIR AND SPACE MUSEUM

Pier 86, W Forty-Sixth Street, New York, NY 10036

The *Intrepid*, a decommissioned World War II aircraft carrier that saw action in the Pacific Theater and Vietnam, became the site of a maritime and flight museum in 1982 when NYC real estate developers saved it from scrap and opened it as a museum on the East River. It's a place to marvel at the wonders of transportation in the city.

Planes, trains, and automobiles!

LA: PETERSEN AUTOMOTIVE MUSEUM

6060 Wilshire Boulevard, Los Angeles, CA 90036

Magazine publisher and car enthusiast Robert E. Petersen founded this museum in 1994 as a site to explore the history of the automobile. In 2015, its building received a face-lift by architects at Kohn Pedersen Fox and was transformed into a now-iconic facade on the corner of Fairfax and Wilshire. It features more than three hundred cars.

NYC: MMUSEUMM

4 Cortlandt Alley, New York, NY 10013

Housed in a freight elevator that holds just three guests at once, this self-described "modern natural history museum" displays objects commonly "overlooked, dismissed, or ignored," like the shoe thrown at George W. Bush at the Minister's Palace in Baghdad. It's unusual to say the least.

Progressive, postmodern, cutting-edge, and trippy museums for curious minds.

LA: MUSEUM OF JURASSIC TECHNOLOGY

9341 Venice Boulevard, Culver City, CA 90232

Often described as a "museum about museums," the Museum of Jurassic Technology feels like a Renaissance "cabinet of curiosity" upon first glance, featuring an odd and eclectic mix of exhibits all with varying degrees of veracity. The museum exists somewhere between poetry and science and provides a mind-bending experience for curious visitors.

NYC: NEW MUSEUM

235 Bowery, New York, NY 10002

One of the few museums worldwide exclusively dedicated to new artwork, the New Museum shows contemporary works from across the globe in ever-changing exhibits.

Art by living artists.

LA: THE BROAD

221 S Grand Avenue, Los Angeles, CA 90012

Housing approximately two thousand pieces of art that billionaire philanthropists Eli and Edythe Broad amassed with the belief that art collections should be acquired while the art is being made, the Broad museum now exists as a veritable temple to contemporary and modern art in downtown Los Angeles.

NYC: THE GUGGENHEIM

1071 Fifth Avenue, New York, NY 10128

In 1943, Hilla Rebay, the director of the nascent Museum of Non-Objective Painting, as Solomon R. Guggenheim's collection was then known, wrote to famed contemporary architect Frank Lloyd Wright requesting a "temple of spirit, a monument!" to house the collection. It took more than sixteen years, but in the autumn of 1959, the spiral building on Manhattan's Upper East Side opened to the public. In the interim, its primary benefactor, Solomon R. Guggenheim, passed away, leading to the museum's renaming in his honor. The building became a National Historic Landmark in 2008.

Great architecture, wealthy namesake founders.

LA: THE GETTY CENTER

1200 Getty Center Drive, Los Angeles, CA 90049

When billionaire oil magnate J. Paul Getty died in 1976, most of his personal wealth went into a museum trust. In 1981, the trust's board hired Harold M. Williams to oversee it and determine how best to manage the extravagant sum within the trust. The trust purchased a massive hilltop parcel of land for its future building in 1983 and hired architect Richard Meier to design the space shortly thereafter. The museum— a blinding white and sharply geometric masterpiece— finally opened in 1997.

NYC: MUSEUM OF MODERN ART

11 W Fifty-Third Street, New York, NY 10019

Founded by Abby Aldrich Rockefeller, Lillie P. Bliss, and Mary Quinn Sullivan in 1929, the MoMa quickly became a hub for modern art from across the globe, championing pioneers from Picasso to Warhol ever since. It's often noted as being one of the premiere modern art institutions in the world.

Modern art hubs.

LA: MUSEUM OF CONTEMPORARY ART

250 S Grand Avenue, Los Angeles, CA 90012

Though it opened nearly half a century after MoMa, in 1983, MOCA quickly rose to prominence as a leading contemporary art institution, propelled by a series of gifts from local collectors. Since then, it has continued to promote pioneering artists and remains a leading cultural institution in the city.

NYC: CITY RELIQUARY

370 Metropolitan Avenue, Brooklyn, NY 11211

Started in 2002 out of founder Dave Herman's apartment, this unique museum showcases relics and artifacts, as well as some odds and ends, from New York City's quotidian history.

Weird little city-history museums.

LA: VALLEY RELICS MUSEUM

7900 Balboa Boulevard, C3 & C4 Entrance on Stagg Street,

Van Nuys, CA 91406

The work of passionate collector Tommy Gelinas, the Valley Relics Museum showcases cultural artifacts—matchbooks, neon signs, restaurant menus—from the region.

LANDMARKS & MONUMENTS

When you think of how to define a city, you might think of its people or its history or its culture...but what do you picture? The collection of landmarks and monuments that compose it.

> **"MANY OF AMERICA'S AND NEW YORK'S SONS AND DAUGHTERS ARE AROUND THE WORLD FIGHTING FOR THE FREEDOMS THAT THE STATUE OF LIBERTY STANDS FOR."**

—Michael Bloomberg

> **"BEING FROM NEW YORK, THERE'S THREE THINGS YOU KNOW ABOUT HOLLYWOOD. YOU KNOW ABOUT THE HOLLYWOOD SIGN, SUNSET STRIP, AND HOLLYWOOD BOULEVARD WITH THE STARS."**

—Sean Combs

NYC: THE STATUE OF LIBERTY

Liberty Island, New York, NY 10004

Since its dedication in 1886, the Statue of Liberty has stood as a symbol for the American spirit of freedom. At 305 feet and 6 inches from the ground to the torch—and a whopping 377 spiral steps up from the main lobby to the crown—it allows for spectacular views of all of New York City.

Pro Tip:

Statue Cruises is the only company granted official permission to ferry tourists to the Statue and provide tours of the pedestal and crown. Tickets must be purchased in advance.

Icons of the skyline with unmatched views of the city.

LA: GRIFFITH OBSERVATORY

2800 E Observatory Road, Los Angeles, CA 90027

An icon of the city since 1935, the Griffith Observatory sits 1,134 feet above sea level atop Mount Hollywood within the expansive Griffith Park. Considering the fact that more people have looked through its telescope than any other telescope on Earth, the observatory inspires wonder and encapsulates the spirit of American adventure—plus, it's a perfect vantage point for the best views of the city, from downtown to the Santa Monica Bay to the Hollywood Sign.

NYC: ONE TIMES SQUARE

1475 Broadway, New York, NY 10036

The site of the annual New Year's Eve ball drop since Adolph Ochs, publisher of the *New York Times* and the building's original building owner, premiered the spectacular event in 1908, One Times Square has served as the focal point—and advertising hub—for the "crossroads of the world," as Times Square has been called. Ochs commissioned the building in 1903 as the headquarters for the *Times*, and upon its completion, then Mayor George B. McClellan renamed the area after it.

Pop culture, entertainment capitals, and tourist mainstays.

LA: HOLLYWOOD WALK OF FAME

Hollywood Boulevard & N Highland Avenue

In 1953, E. M. Stuart, the president of the Hollywood Chamber of Commerce, thought of the name "Walk of Fame" in order to "maintain the glory of a community whose name means glamour and excitement in the four corners of the world." The first star (of director Stanley Kramer) was unveiled in 1960, and today, Mr. Stuart's goal has been achieved with more than ten million annual visitors flocking to see the 2,600-plus stars on the iconic corner of Hollywood Boulevard and North Highland Avenue.

NYC: WASHINGTON SQUARE ARCH

Washington Square N, New York, NY 10012

Designed by famed architect Stanford White and erected in 1892 to celebrate the centennial of George Washington's inauguration as president, the Washington Square Arch stands at the base of Fifth Avenue on the northern border of Washington Square Park in the heart of Greenwich Village. Since as early as 1911, when labor unions marched through the Arch, it has long been a site for political protests as well as a gathering place for avant-garde musicians and artists. Nowadays, the arch instantly brings to mind the spirit and vibe of downtown Manhattan, as evidenced by its cameos in countless NYC-based films.

Welcome signs for popular neighborhoods.

LA: SANTA MONICA PIER SIGN

200 Santa Monica Pier, Santa Monica, CA 90401

Arching over the entrance to the Santa Monica Pier at the intersection of Colorado and Ocean Avenues, the Santa Monica Pier sign glows in an iconic neon that epitomizes the Streamline Moderne, or late art deco, style from the surrounding decade from when it was erected in 1941. The pier itself achieved National Landmark status in 1976, and in the countless movies and TV shows in which its seen, it symbolizes the endless summer and West Coast feeling of the city.

NYC: RADIO CITY MUSIC HALL

1260 Sixth Avenue, New York, NY 10020

Built as part of the enormous Rockefeller Center complex in the 1930s, Radio City Music Hall had its first show on December 27, 1932, in what was the world's largest auditorium at the time. It's an icon of art deco style and still operates as a musical venue to this day.

Shrines of entertainment.

LA: EGYPTIAN THEATRE

6712 Hollywood Boulevard, Los Angeles, CA 90028

Opened in 1922 and the home of the first-ever Hollywood film premiere, the Egyptian Theatre was Sid Grauman's first "movie palace." He later opened the Chinese Theatre down the block, which perhaps today rivals the Egyptian's fame, but both still operate as movie theaters to this day.

NYC: BROOKLYN BRIDGE

New York, NY 10038

With a spiderweb of cords stretching between two massive pillars, the Brooklyn Bridge straddles the East River, connecting Manhattan and Brooklyn. Architect and engineer John Augustus Roebling planned the bridge for nearly fifteen years until his death in 1869, when his son Washington Roebling inherited the project and embarked on another nearly fifteen years of construction. It is the first steel-wire suspension bridge ever constructed and has been an indelible icon of the city for more than 130 years.

Gigantic and unforgettable.

LA: HOLLYWOOD SIGN

Los Angeles, CA 90068

The sign originally read "Hollywoodland" to advertise *Los Angeles Times* publisher Harry Chandler's new upscale real estate development in 1923, but the city removed the "land" portion in 1949. The following decades led to deterioration of the sign until a benefit spearheaded by Hugh Hefner and other celebrities in 1978 brought it newfound glory. It now stands as a glimmering beacon and banner for the entertainment capital of the world.

NYC: CHRYSLER BUILDING

405 Lexington Avenue, New York, NY 10174

The Chrysler Building stood as the world's tallest building upon its completion in 1930—but the accolade only lasted eleven months, until the Empire State Building opened its doors. Both buildings were the result of a fierce competition among successful businessmen in New York in the 1920s to build the city's largest structures. Even though Walter Chrysler, the chairman of the Chrysler Motor Company, lost the race for tallest, his William Van Alen–designed structure is widely regarded as one of the most beautiful buildings in the world, a shining example of art deco architecture and a symbol of Midtown Manhattan.

Icons of style, not height.

LA: CAPITOL RECORDS BUILDING

1750 Vine Street, Los Angeles, CA 90028

Famed Los Angeles architect Welton Becket and an associate at his firm named Louis Naidorf designed the West Coast headquarters for Capital Records in 1955, creating one of the first-ever circular buildings and a mid-century masterpiece. Standing only fourteen stories tall, it makes up for its lack of height with its iconic design.

NYC: ALICE IN WONDERLAND

Seventy-Sixth Street and Fifth Avenue, near Conservatory Lake

George Delacorte founded Dell Publishers as a response to the uptight and formal nature of books and magazines of his time. Its most successful innovation became its puzzle books. Delacorte amassed a fortune, then dedicated much of his attention the beautification of New York City, albeit with his irreverent style. In the 1950s, he commissioned Spanish sculptor Jose de Creeft to build a tribute to Lewis Carroll's Alice in Wonderland to be displayed in Central Park. The whimsical statue was dedicated on May 7, 1959, and has ever since been a lasting tribute to the weird, wild, and whimsical.

Eccentric public artwork.

LA: WATTS TOWERS

1727 E 107th Street, Los Angeles, CA 90002

In 1921, an Italian immigrant named Sabato "Simon" Rodia began collecting scrap metal, glass, tile, seashells, and other miscellaneous debris with the intention of making "something big." He started assembling his materials, slowly building a series of formations on his small property in the neighborhood of Watts, eventually becoming full-fledged towers with the highest stretching nearly one hundred feet. Over the next thirty years, he continued to build the amazing structure on his own with little to no fanfare. Yet after his death in 1965, the compilation has become known as one of the preeminent "outsider artworks" in the world.

NYC: STEPHEN A. SCHWARZMAN BUILDING, NEW YORK PUBLIC LIBRARY

476 Fifth Avenue, New York, NY 10018

With more than 125 miles of books—that's about 53 million collection items—the New York Public Library has one of the greatest collections in the world. Its massive headquarter building in Midtown Manhattan stands proud as a symbol of the city's intellect and spirit.

The spirit of the city.

LA: L.A. LIVE

800 West Olympic Boulevard, Los Angeles, CA 90015

With more than 5.6 million square feet dedicated to entertainment—with attractions including theaters, ballrooms, restaurants, bars, shopping, a 7,000-seat concert hall, the Grammy museum, JW Marriott and Ritz Carlton Hotels, a fourteen-screen Regal cinema complex, and much more— L.A. Live is as sprawling entertainment complex that only Los Angeles could require. It's expansive, shiny, flashy, and, in many ways, epitomizes the spirit of Los Angeles.

NYC: THE HIGH LINE

New York, NY 10011

The city built an elevated train around 1943, but after forty
years of use, the trains all but ceased to run, as modern-day
trucking took its functional place. Throughout the 1980s and
'90s, the track faced possible demolition many times, but
in 1999, two New York residents, Joshua David and Robert
Hammond, founded a nonprofit called Friends of the
High Line to help transform and preserve the space.
The High Line now stretches 1.45 miles from Gansevoort
and Washington Streets (near the Whitney Museum),
with several entrance points along the way, to Thirty-Fourth
Street and Eleventh Avenue and provides gorgeous
recreation space for millions of visitors a year.

Nice walks and great views in hip neighborhoods.

LA: MARVIN BRAUDE BIKE TRAIL, A.K.A. THE STRAND

Most simply described as "the bike path at the beach," the
Strand curves along the coast, stretching from the Pacific
Palisades down to Torrance and covering about twenty-two
miles. Former councilman Marvin Braude (the same man who
pushed for a smoking ban—twice!—until it passed in 1991)
proposed the path in the 1960s, but it wasn't until 1988 that
it opened. Along the path you'll find surfers, muscle builders,
volleyball players, tattoo artists, buskers, trinket peddlers,
dogs, teenagers, skaters, and some of the best, most iconic
beach views in the country.

NYC: GRAND CENTRAL TERMINAL

89 E Forty-Second Street, New York, NY 10017

The symbolic center of New York City opened its doors in 1913 after a decade-long process, including a design competition that led to two different winners who ended up combining designs. The resulting structure is a beaux arts masterpiece as stunning as it is functional. The building achieved official landmark status in 1978 only after former First Lady Jacqueline Kennedy Onassis and architect Philip Johnson led a charge to save the terminal from destruction by developers. Colloquially called "Grand Central Station" by many, Grand Central Terminal is its official name.

Iconic transportation hubs.

LA: UNION STATION

800 N Alameda Street, Los Angeles, CA 90012

In the 1930s, as train travel hit peak popularity in Southern California, the dominant train operators, including Southern Pacific, Union Pacific, and Atchison, Topeka, and Santa Fe railroads, combined forces to open a central hub. Union Station opened its doors in 1939 with a unique combination of Spanish colonial, mission revival, and art deco architecture, which came to be known as "Mission Moderne." The station still operates similarly to how it did upon opening.

NYC: TRINITY CHURCH

75 Broadway, New York, NY 10006

Established in 1696, Trinity Church has been serving New Yorkers since long before the birth of the USA. Beside its chapel, at the corner of Broadway and Wall Street, sits a historic graveyard, containing numerous Revolutionary War heroes and early New Yorkers as well as the grave of the $10-bill man himself, Alexander Hamilton.

Celebrate the macabre.

LA: HOLLYWOOD FOREVER CEMETERY

6000 Santa Monica Boulevard, Los Angeles, CA 90038

Founded in 1899, the Hollywood Forever Cemetery sits behind Paramount Pictures and houses the graves of some of the most iconic stars, including Rudolph Valentino, Judy Garland, Mickey Rooney, and Douglas Fairbanks. It also hosts events, such as readings, concerts, and a famous film screening series.

NYC: 9/11 MEMORIAL & MUSEUM

180 Greenwich Street, New York, NY 10007

Opening to the public thirteen years after the devastating attacks on the World Trade Center, the museum and memorial built on the archeological site reminds the world of the city's resilience and spirit in the aftermath of the horror.

Critical city history.

LA: EL PUEBLO DE LOS ANGELES

125 Paseo De La Plaza, Los Angeles, CA 90012

The historic center of Los Angeles and the birthplace of the city, this hub of buildings and streets represents a protected cultural landmark celebrating the city's Mexican roots.

ARCHITECTURE

We've discussed important monuments, historic sites, and cultural landmarks, but what about architecture on its own? Architecture for architecture's sake? Here's a look at some notable buildings on either coast:

NEW YORK

LOS ANGELES

THE DAKOTA

*1 W Seventy-Second Street,
New York, NY 10023*

Henry J. Hardenbergh, architect of the Plaza Hotel, designed this National Historic Landmark that gained international fame for being the final residence of John Lennon.

THE STAHL HOUSE (CASE STUDY HOUSE #22)

*1635 Woods Drive,
Los Angeles, CA 90069*

The "Arts & Architecture" Case Study series, which commissioned emerging modernist architecture in Southern California, has become cemented as a classic of refined style and minimalist design in part by architect Pierre Koenig's Hollywood Hills home. You've likely seen the iconic Julius Shulman photo of the house; it has come to define midcentury life and glamour in Los Angeles.

"WHIMSICAL HOUSE"

75 1/2 Bedford Street,
New York, NY 10014

At only 9.5 feet wide, this cartoonishly small house went up in 1873 and has had a series of fittingly whimsical residents, including a candy factory, then later the home of *New Yorker* cartoonist (and creator of *Shrek*) William Steig.

"WHIMSICAL BUILDING"

255 Main Street,
Venice, CA 90291

The "ballerina clown" with a five o'clock shadow has overlooked Main Street in Santa Monica since sculptor Jonathan Borofsky unveiled his creation in 1989. It's thirty feet tall and stands on a large crate above the entrance to a CVS Pharmacy.

"TALLEST RESIDENTIAL BUILDING"

432 Park Avenue Skyscraper,
New York, NY 10022

Rafael Viñoly's 432 Park Avenue has become known as "the billionaire's middle finger" due to its unfortunate placement at the base of Central Park, design, and exorbitant prices.

"LARGEST RESIDENCE"

Spelling Manor,
594 S Mapleton Drive,
Los Angeles, CA 90024

Billionaire Aaron Spelling purchased Bing Crosby's former estate on a six-acre property and demolished it to build the largest house in Los Angeles County. It boasts 56,500 square feet, seventeen bedrooms, thirty bathrooms, a bowling alley, a one-hundred-car garage, and an entire floor devoted to closets.

"JENGA BUILDING"

56 Leonard Street,
New York, NY 10013

Herzog & de Meuron's glass Jenga building, described by the famed architects as "houses stacked upon one another" presents a dizzying sight in downtown Manhattan.

"BINOCULARS BUILDING"

340 Main Street,
Venice, CA 90291

Now occupied by Google but originally built as the West Coast headquarters of the ad agency Chiat/Day, the Venice Binoculars Building is literally that: a facade in the shape of a massive set of binoculars designed by famed artists Claes Oldenburg and Coosje van Bruggen and connected to a Frank Gehry building.

THE ANSONIA

2109 Broadway,
New York, NY 10023

Built in 1904, it used to have a farm on its roof to deliver fresh eggs to its tenants. It also featured one of the first air-conditioning systems in the city and a gay club in its basement. Now, it's one of many beautiful turn-of-the-century buildings near Manhattan's Central Park with a strange history.

THE SPADENA HOUSE

516 Walden Drive,
Beverly Hills, CA 90210

This little cottage in Beverly Hills looks like something straight out of a Grimms' fairy tale. It's affectionately known as the "Witch's House" and was built by a revered film production designer named Harry Oliver. It was originally used as a dressing room on a film studio lot but was moved to its Beverly Hills location in 1934.

HESS ESTATE SIDEWALK SQUARE

There are 500 square inches in Greenwich Village with a plaque on the ground that says, "Property of the Hess Estate Which Has Never Been Dedicated for Public Purposes." Yup, pretty cool to own a little, itty-bitty piece of New York sidewalk.

THE CHEMOSPHERE

7776 Torreyson Drive, Los Angeles, CA 90046

John Edward Lautner, a Frank Lloyd Wright protégé, designed this house, which was completed in 1960. Decades later, the Taschen family took ownership and threw decadent parties there.

THE WYCKOFF HOUSE

5816 Clarendon Road, Brooklyn, NY 11203

The Wyckoff House is a farmhouse that was built around 1652 and still stands in Brooklyn.

LA PLACITA CHURCH

535 N Main Street, Los Angeles, CA 90012

La Placita Church is believed to have been constructed in 1818, around the same time as when the nearby Avila Adobe went up, which backs up its claim of being the oldest building in Los Angeles.

HOTELS

Eloise stayed at the Plaza. Vivian Ward (Julia Roberts in *Pretty Woman*) stayed at the Beverly Wilshire. Hotels can define a city. It's how a city welcomes its guests and where visitors call home. Where can you find the best, most unusual, and historic hotels in either place?

NEW YORK

LOS ANGELES

WASHINGTON SQUARE HOTEL

103 Waverly Place, New York, NY 10011

With an aesthetic and history that defines downtown cool, the hotel is perched just steps from Washington Square Park and known as a place where Bob Dylan lived twice.

CHATEAU MARMONT

8221 Sunset Boulevard, Los Angeles, CA 90046

What celebrity hasn't taken up residence in this private party haven?

THE PLAZA

768 Fifth Avenue, New York, NY 10019

The hotel made famous as the home of the legendary children's book character Eloise.

BEVERLY HILLS HOTEL

9641 Sunset Boulevard, Beverly Hills, CA 90210

The oldest hotel in Beverly Hills and to this day an emblem of the city.

THE CARLYLE

*35 E Seventy-Sixth Street,
New York, NY 10021*

It's an elegant New York institution that has been known as "the New York White House," since JFK kept an apartment there during his presidency.

MILLENNIUM BILTMORE HOTEL

*506 S Grand Avenue,
Los Angeles, CA 90071*

Upon its opening in 1923, it was the largest hotel west of Chicago. It was the site of JFK's acceptance speech as the Democratic nominee in 1960 and feels like downtown's crown, with its regal and over-the-top elegance and design.

THE MARK HOTEL

*25 E Seventy-Seventh Street,
New York, NY 10075*

Famous for being the place many celebrities get ready for the annual Met Gala.

BEVERLY HILTON

*9876 Wilshire Boulevard,
Beverly Hills, CA 90210*

It boasts a long history as the home of the annual Golden Globes.

THE JANE HOTEL

*113 Jane Street,
New York, NY 10014*

It's well known as having one of the coolest bars in the city, with famous DJs hosting sets, exclusive rooftop parties, and a sort of private club vibe.

SUNSET TOWER

*8358 Sunset Boulevard,
Los Angeles, CA 90069*

Perhaps the hotel on the Strip that epitomizes old-world Hollywood glamour—and is well known as one of the coolest bars in the city.

ALGONQUIN HOTEL

*59 W Forty-Fourth Street,
New York, NY 10036*

Well known as a literary hangout in the early twentieth century and where the *New Yorker* was founded.

THE HOLLYWOOD ROOSEVELT

*7000 Hollywood Boulevard,
Los Angeles, CA 90028*

Opened in 1929, it's the oldest continuously operated hotel in Los Angeles, full of Hollywood history: Marilyn Monroe lived in it for two years, and it hosted the first-ever Oscars in 1929.

NEW YORKER HOTEL

*481 Eighth Avenue,
New York, NY 10001*

It's a classic, old-school hotel (where Ali recovered after losing to Joe Frazier), with an iconic sign looming over Midtown.

BEVERLY WILSHIRE

*9500 Wilshire Boulevard,
Beverly Hills, CA 90212*

At the heart of Beverly Hills since its opening 1928, it was the home for many years of Elvis Presley and Warren Beatty as well as the primary setting for the film *Pretty Woman*.

THE PIERRE

2 East Sixty-First Street & Fifth Avenue, New York, NY 10065

It's the height of old-world elegance on Central Park, with regal decor and top-notch service.

SHUTTERS

*1 Pico Boulevard,
Santa Monica, CA 90405*

It's the pinnacle of classic luxury on the beach, with unmatched access to the Pacific Ocean.

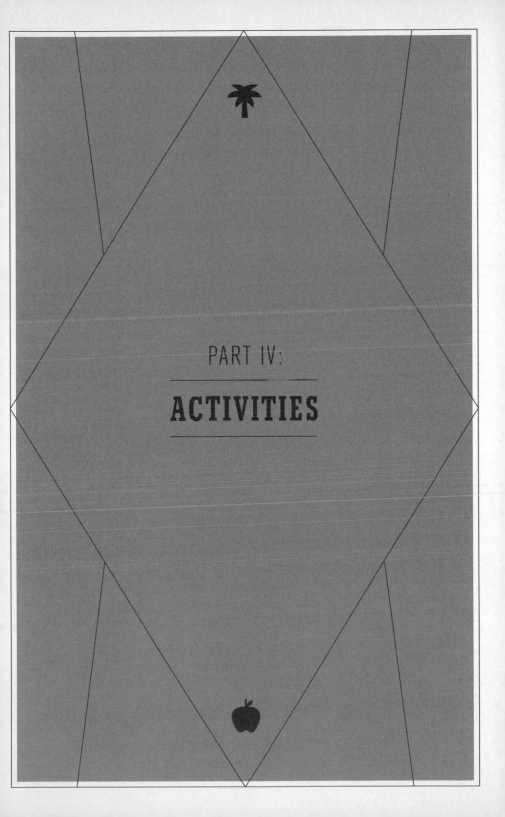

PART IV:

ACTIVITIES

How do New Yorkers and Angelenos spend their time? Each city offers endless sources of activities to occupy your days. You'd be hard pressed to be bored on either coast.

FITNESS & THE OUTDOORS

New York cherishes its many green parks as escapes from its dense mass of concrete and buildings. Los Angeles doesn't suffer from such a congestion of metal, glass, and steel. Instead, its sprawling nature allows for plenty of green, grass, and trees across its geography. Still, Angelenos long for an escape of their own, something different from the everyday sights, and they find it in the long coastline of beaches from Ventura County line down to the O.C.

NEW YORK: PARKS   LOS ANGELES: BEACHES

PROSPECT PARK

Prospect Park W, Parkside Avenue between Flatbush Avenue, Ocean Avenue, and Prospect Park SW

Big, practical, and widely considered to be Frederick Law Olmsted and Calvert B. Vaux's masterpiece—even though they also built the more famous Central Park—it offers a diverse landscape with ample room for all imaginable activities in the heart of Brooklyn.

ZUMA BEACH

30050 Pacific Coast Highway, Malibu, CA 90265

The wide spread of sand provides an incredible setting and ample space for all activities from Frisbee to volleyball, while the water itself hosts tons of surfers and swimmers, both tourists and locals alike.

JAMAICA BAY WILDLIFE REFUGE

Cross Bay Blvd near Broad Channel Queens, NY 11693

Famous for its massive bird sanctuary, this South Brooklyn expanse attracts wildlife lovers from across the state.

LEO CARRILLO STATE BEACH

35000 Pacific Coast Highway, Malibu, CA 90265

An ecological wonderland, this North Malibu enclave is famous for its myriad of tide pools and diverse sea life.

CENTRAL PARK

From 59th Street to 110th Street, between Fifth Avenue and Central Park West

The most iconic park in the nation (perhaps in the world?), it is also among the most visited parks in the world and most frequently referred to as simply "the Park."

SANTA MONICA STATE BEACH

Pacific Coast Highway, Santa Monica, CA 90401

It's what you imagine when you picture California: palm trees, bikinis, a surreal sunset. It's the most iconic beach in the state, with the famous pier and spinning Ferris wheel in its backdrop.

FORT TYRON PARK

Riverside Drive to Broadway, W 192 Street to Dyckman Street

Situated at the very northern tip of Manhattan, this hidden gem features stunning views of the George Washington Bridge, ample greenery, and the famous Met Cloisters.

EL MATADOR

32350 Pacific Coast Highway, Malibu, CA 90265

The picturesque Malibu beach features the famous arch rock formation from *The Notebook* and Madonna's "Cherish" and Miley Cyrus's "Malibu" music videos.

WASHINGTON SQUARE PARK

Fifth Avenue, Waverly Place, W Fourth Street and MacDougal Street

With a long history of protests and Greenwich Village counterculture, it's perhaps New York's funkiest park.

VENICE BEACH

3100–2700 Ocean Front Walk, Venice, CA 90291

Graffiti, street artists, tattoo parlors, and lots of marijuana, this counterculture haven has been a prime surf spot in Southern California for decades.

In addition to these amazing beaches, check out these top surf spots along the coast!

LOS ANGELES

◆

COUNTY LINE

Sublime setting at the northernmost edge of the Los Angeles county line.

LEO CARRILLO

Good for all levels, short- and longboarders.

SURFRIDER BEACH

Perhaps the most iconic beach in California (maybe the USA?) for being an early hub of the sport.

TOPANGA

Dangerous rocky bottom makes it less congested, but with fierce waves.

SUNSET

Mellow, rolling waves perfect for longboarding, but no sand beach.

VENICE

Claims to be the origin spot for shortboarding and infamous for its "locals-only" culture.

EL PORTO

Can get gnarly in the winter, and you can spot pros here from time to time.

But don't feel left out if you're in New York! Sure, you can surf out in the Rockaways or on Long Island, but for a more accessible watersport, you can find ample spots to boat along the coast:

NEW YORK

BROOKLYN BRIDGE PARK–PIER 2

An eastside pier to boat in the East River.

LONG ISLAND CITY COMMUNITY BOATHOUSE

46-01 Fifth Street, Long Island City, NY 11101

Embark from Queens to boat in the East River.

RED HOOK BOATERS

Louis Valentino Jr. Pier Park, Coffey Street and Ferris Street, Brooklyn, NY 11231

Rent a boat from a Brooklyn hipster enclave.

HUDSON RIVER PARK–PIERS 26 AND 96

Classic launching points on the west side of Manhattan.

BRIDGES & STAIRCASES

Manhattan's an island with many bridges; Los Angeles is a sprawling mess, built on a diverse mix of landscapes. As a result, Manhattan has many famous bridges while LA has famous staircases.

NEW YORK: BRIDGES

HIGH BRIDGE

The oldest bridge in New York, opened in 1948, stretches 1,450 feet and features a tower on the Manhattan (Harlem) side. It was restored in 2015 and only allows pedestrians.

WARDS ISLAND BRIDGE

Stretching 1,247 feet, with a unique blue sapphire color, this 12-foot-wide bridge transports pedestrians and cyclists (no cars or trains) from Manhattan to the tiny Wards Island.

LOS ANGELES: STAIRCASES

DRAKE STADIUM—A.K.A. THE UCLA STAIRS

*340 Bruin Walk,
Los Angeles, CA 90095*

An Olympic-size track on the gorgeous UCLA campus, open to the public for recreation, you can work out next to international track-and-field stars on the track loop itself, but the more popular workout has to be ascending the bleacher steps again and again.

BUNKER HILL STAIRS

*633 W Fifth Street,
Los Angeles, CA 90071*

101 steps located in the center of downtown LA.

MANHATTAN BRIDGE

Stretching an amazing 6,854 feet from Manhattan to Brooklyn, it originally carried the title "Bridge 3," as it was the third bridge to open across the East River when it was completed in 1909.

THE SANTA MONICA STAIRS—A.K.A. THE ENTRADA STAIRS OR THE SEVENTH STREET STAIRS

Entrada Drive & Amalfi Drive, Santa Monica, CA 90402

A pair of staircases—one wooden and the other concrete, 170 and 189 steps respectively—about a half mile from the Pacific Ocean, tucked away among multimillion-dollar properties.

GEORGE WASHINGTON BRIDGE

The primary commuter bridge over the Hudson River, connecting NY to NJ, the city charges an obscene toll of $12.50 during peak hours!

BEACHWOOD CANYON STAIRS

2695 N Beachwood Drive, Los Angeles, CA. 90068

These stairs have more than five hundred steps that wind and loop through the original Hollywoodland housing development, where stars like Busby Berkeley, Humphrey Bogart, and Bela Lugosi lived.

WILLIAMSBURG BRIDGE

It stretches 7,308 feet across the East River and features two signs written by Brooklyn borough president Marty Markowitz: on one end it says, "Leaving Brooklyn: Oy vey!" and, on the other end, "Leaving Brooklyn, Fuhgeddaboudit!"

MUSIC BOX STAIRS

3278 Descanso Drive, Los Angeles, CA 90026

These 706 steps were immortalized by the Oscar-winning Laurel & Hardy short film in which the duo attempt to transport a piano up the staircase to great comic affect.

CARROLL STREET BRIDGE

Stretching over the Gowanus Canal at only 300 feet high, it remarkably has been designated as an official city landmark since it's only one of four retractable bridges in the nation and remains the least-used vehicular bridge in all of the city.

CASTELLAMMARE STAIRS— A.K.A. THE PACIFIC PALISADES STAIRS

17606 Posetano Drive, Los Angeles, CA 90272

Perhaps the most stunning set of stairs in the city, with continuous views of the Pacific Ocean and Malibu.

QUEENSBORO BRIDGE

Officially the Ed Koch Queensboro Bridge but more commonly known as the Fifty-Ninth Street Bridge—and the grueling mile 15 of the NYC Marathon—this 3,724-foot-long bridge connects Queens with Manhattan and is a true behemoth.

BAXTER STREET STAIRS— A.K.A. THE ECHO PARK STAIRS

1501 Baxter Street, Los Angeles, CA 90026

With claims as the steepest staircases in Los Angeles and with 231 steps, this Elysian Park path is a beast to climb.

BROOKLYN BRIDGE

Spanning the East River at 5,988 feet long, the truly iconic masterpiece is the world's oldest suspension bridge and, despite being overcrowded with tourists, is still a blast to traverse.

BALDWIN HILLS SCENIC OVERLOOK—A.K.A. THE CULVER CITY STAIRS

6300 Hetzler Road, Culver City, CA 90232

With 282 steps and winding its way through a historic park, this path provides a scenic overlook of the whole city with 360-degree views.

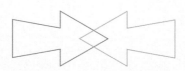

BIKES & HIKES

Angelenos love to hike. Or, at the very least, they love to call casual walks up moderately steep hills, oftentimes evenly paved, "hikes," as if they're trekking into the wilderness. Ever been to Runyon Canyon? You'll see guys in jeans and girls in leather jackets routinely next to your out-of-work actor running shirtless hoping to catch the eye of a casting director. That said, it's pretty spectacular to have so much nature—no matter how tamed—interspersed throughout the city.

New York doesn't offer the same opportunity to "hike" within its borders. Yet New Yorkers seems to love an equally athletic activity nearly as much: bike riding. The Central Park Loop has long been a destination for serious cyclists, while the Hudson River Greenway on the Westside Highway has become a must for tourists and locals during the summer. Citi Bike premiered in 2013 to much fanfare allowing casual riders to pick up a bike nearly anywhere in the city and providing a simple alternative to public transportation.

NEW YORK: BIKE

LOS ANGELES: HIKE

STATEN ISLAND GREENBELT BLUE TRAIL

2.6 miles

Winding trail through a massive park on Staten Island and accessible via ferry from Manhattan.

TEMESCAL CANYON LOOP

(Pacific Palisades)

Minutes from the center of the chic Palisades town center, this path is easily accessible and easy to hike.

HUDSON RIVER GREENWAY—A.K.A. WESTSIDE HIGHWAY PATH AND PARK

11 miles

This pristine cyclist and pedestrian path runs along the West Side of Manhattan from its southernmost tip (Battery Park) up to the George Washington Bridge.

RUNYON CANYON

(Hollywood)
approx. 2 miles long

This trail is often called a glorified dog park for its parade of fancy pups and an open casting call because of its constant parade of shirtless aspiring models.

JAMAICA BAY GREENWAY —A.K.A. THE ROCKAWAY BIKE PATH

19 miles

Loop around Rockaway Beach, Jacob Riis Park, Canarsie Pier, and through the Jamaica Bay Wildlife Refuge on this path, installed in 2012.

CORRAL CANYON—A.K.A. SOLSTICE CANYON TRAIL

(Malibu)
approx. 2.5 miles

Extending off the Pacific Coastal Highway, this trail offers unparalleled views of the ocean and an all-seasons waterfall.

ROOSEVELT ISLAND GREENWAY

3.8 miles

Ride the elevated tramway over the Hudson River and explore a historic "Lunatic Asylum" and the new $2-billion, two-million-square-foot Cornell Tech Campus.

BRIDGE TO NOWHERE

10 miles (there and back)

Features plenty of swimming holes, scenic overlooks, and a deserted bridge along an abandoned highway trail.

CENTRAL PARK LOOP

6 miles

Bikers can enjoy three different long-distance routes and weave around various paths throughout the park, but the six-mile outer perimeter provides a classic view of the entire park and remains popular for joggers as well.

INSPIRATION LOOP TRAIL

(Will Rogers Park, Pacific Palisades)
approx. 2 miles

An easy loop with stunning views of the Westside of the city.

OCEAN PARKWAY BIKE PATH

5.5 miles

The country's first bike path runs from the southern tip of Prospect Park to Coney Island and was designed in part by Frederick Law Olmsted, the mastermind behind Central and Prospect Parks.

MOUNT HOLLYWOOD TRAIL

(Griffith Park, Los Felix)
approx. 3 miles

This winding dirt road up to Griffith Observatory leads to outstanding views of the Hollywood sign and most of Los Angeles.

GOVERNORS ISLAND

2 miles

Tour this historic island just eight hundred yards off the tip of Manhattan (accessible only by ferry), which was a historic Revolutionary War strategic site and originally called "nut island."

FRYMAN CANYON

(Studio City)
3 miles

Chock full of Lululemon, oversize sunglasses, and shirtless men, this hike's more scene-y than scenic, but still good for some quick exercise.

SWIMMING POOLS

Stuck in New York's intolerable summer heat without a place to escape out east on the beach? No worries, because the city has an incredible collection of public pools across all its neighborhoods. And, of course, in Los Angeles, you can seek out a spot on the seventy miles of pristine beaches along the Pacific to escape the heat. But when those beaches fill up with tourists, you ought not feel stranded: LA has its own incredible collection of public swimming pools to cool you down.

NEW YORK

LOS ANGELES

TONY DAPOLITO RECREATION CENTER

4330, 1 Clarkson Street,
New York, NY 10014

Swim beneath an authentic Keith Haring mural.

CULVER CITY PLUNGE

4175 Overland Avenue,
Culver City, CA 90230

Large and nicely maintained with a central location.

MCCARREN PARK POOL

776 Lorimer Street,
Brooklyn, NY 11222

Hipsters in swimsuits.

STONER PARK

1835 Stoner Avenue,
Los Angeles, CA 90025

A wading pool no deeper than four feet, but a quirky way to cool off in summer months.

ASTORIA POOL

Nineteenth Street & Twenty-Third Drive, Astoria, NY 11105

Opened in 1936, it hosted the final Olympic Trials that year, and its art deco flourishes remain to this day—plus, it has amazing views of the East Side of Manhattan.

HOLLYWOOD RECREATION CENTER

1122 Cole Avenue, Los Angeles, CA 90038

Revamped and refreshed in 2015, it features a modern vibe and a spiral waterslide.

LASKER POOL

Malcolm X Boulevard, New York, NY 10029

Massive and supremely clean within the overwhelming greenery of Central Park.

LA84 FOUNDATION/JOHN C. ARGUE SWIM STADIUM

3980 Bill Robertson Lane, Los Angeles, CA 90037

Built for the 1932 Olympics.

FLOATING POOL

Barretto Point Park, Bronx at Tiffany Street & Viele Avenue

Perhaps the most innovative and clever architecturally of the bunch, this pool opened on an abandoned barge in a remote corner of the Bronx so visitors can actually swim "above" the water on the East River.

HANSEN DAM AQUATIC CENTER

11798 Foothill Boulevard, Lake View Terrace, CA 91342

At the base of the San Gabriel Mountains sits LA's largest pool, which also features a massive waterslide and lake right next door.

HIGHBRIDGE POOL

*2301 Amsterdam Avenue,
New York, NY 10033*

An oasis at the base of the city's oldest bridge, this complex features two separate large pools, which are an easy walk over said bridge from the Bronx.

VERDUGO AQUATIC FACILITY

*3201 W Verdugo Avenue,
Burbank, CA 91505*

A wild, crazy, and imaginative playground and fantastic waterslide make this public pool tough to beat for kids to have a blast on hot summer days.

HAMILTON FISH POOL

*1844, 128 Pitt Street,
New York, NY 10002*

It's named for a former New York governor and secretary of state under Ulysses S. Grant, but is perhaps the most fitting name for a pool in either city.

ANNENBERG COMMUNITY BEACH HOUSE

*415 Pacific Coast Highway,
Santa Monica, CA 90402*

Modern redesign of a former mansion on the sand now open to the public for a modest entry fee.

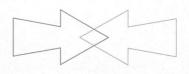

PLAYGROUNDS

Sure, there are plenty of cultural sights to visit, museums to see, and educational experiences to embark upon, but there's also a handful of incredibly creative and exciting playgrounds in either city for children to enjoy:

NEW YORK

THE HILLS AT GOVERNORS ISLAND

870-898 Gresham Road, New York, NY 10004

It features three slides, including one that's more than three stories high—plus, it has epic views of Manhattan.

PIER 6 PLAYGROUND, BROOKLYN HEIGHTS

Brooklyn Bridge Park Greenway, Brooklyn, NY 11201

A combination of five playgrounds on the waterfront near the classic Brooklyn merry-go-round, Jane's Carousel.

LOS ANGELES

LAKE BALBOA/ANTHONY C. BEILENSON PARK

6300 Balboa Boulevard, Van Nuys, CA 91406

It has two different playgrounds covered in shade, with a picturesque lake in the backdrop.

SHANE'S INSPIRATION IN GRIFFITH PARK

4800 Crystal Springs Drive, Los Angeles, CA 90027

This playground sits near the park's iconic merry-go-round (which is well known as being one of Walt Disney's favorite attractions in the city).

ANCIENT PLAYGROUND

Museum Mile,
New York, NY 10028

An Egyptian-themed
jungle gym next to the
Met in Central Park.

REESE'S RETREAT

360 N Arroyo Boulevard,
Pasadena, CA 91103

A pirate-themed
playground behind the
Rose Bowl in Pasadena.

HIPPO PARK
PLAYGROUND

W Ninety-First Street
& Riverside Drive,
New York, NY 10025

A whimsical collection of
hippo statues to tumble
and climb upon.

COSTANSO FIRE STATION
84 PARK

21396 Costanso Street,
Woodland Hills, CA 91364

This Woodland Hills
structure looks like a
fantasy fire engine.

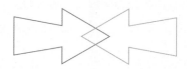

DOG PARKS

French bullbogs rule New York. Chihuahuas rule Los Angeles. Bulldogs, poodles, and Labradors can be found in droves in both places. New Yorkers and Angelenos both love their dogs—and have plenty of amazing options to keep them entertained. Here's a breakdown of the best dog parks:

NEW YORK

SIRIUS DOG RUN

Hudson River Park Pier 40, 353 West Street, New York, NY 10014

The Sirius Dog Run proudly pays homage to a fallen hero, as its named after the only police K-9 to die in the September 11 terror attacks.

WEST VILLAGE D.O.G. RUN

55 Little W Twelfth Street, New York, NY 10014

A members-only park in posh West Village.

LOS ANGELES

ROSIE'S DOG BEACH

4800 E Ocean Boulevard, Long Beach, CA 90803

Some say it's the best officially designated dog park on the beach in Southern California.

BEVERLY HILLS DOG PARK

344 Foothill Road, Beverly Hills, CA 90210

A members-only park in posh Beverly Hills.

TOMPKINS SQUARE DOG RUN

*Avenue B and E Ninth Street,
New York, NY 10009*

This spacious park has a brick-tile floor so it's relatively clean, and it hosts a famous Halloween contest for dogs each year.

ALICE'S DOG PARK

*3026 E Orange Grove
Boulevard,
Pasadena, CA 91107*

A massive dog park with more than two acres of land for pups to run wild.

MADISON SQUARE DOG RUN

*Madison Square Park near
Broadway and Fifth Avenue,
New York, NY 10010*

Conveniently located just north of the iconic Flatiron Building.

LAKE HOLLYWOOD PARK

*3200 Canyon Lake Drive,
Los Angeles, CA 90068*

While it's not technically an off-leash park, this spot's popular for dog owners and features great views of Hollywood.

WASHINGTON SQUARE PARK DOG RUN

*Fifth Avenue, Waverly Place,
West Fourth Street, between
MacDougal and Thompson
Streets, south side of the park
(behind building)*

Some of the best pup (and people) watching in the city.

RUNYON CANYON DOG PARK

*2000 N Fuller Avenue
Los Angeles, CA 90046*

While not technically a dog park, this casual "hike" has become overrun with dogs and remains one of the premier people-watching spots in the city.

BOOKSTORES

Since Henry Holt opened the doors to his book publishing company in 1866, New York City has maintained its status as the epicenter of publishing within the nation, if not the world. It's home to all "big five" publishing houses plus massive magazine publishers Hearst, Condé Nast, Time Inc., and more. The city celebrates its literati image and cherishes its bookstores. On any given night in New York, one can see a Pulitzer winner give a reading from a new work or a Nobel Laureate give a talk.

The other coast may not have the same book publishing pedigree as New York, but it does host all the major movie studios and remains the worldwide center of entertainment. It's a city with a ton of writers—even if they happen to write for the screen, rather than for print. What Angeleno doesn't have a screenplay they've written sitting idle in a desk drawer? Either way, it's no surprise that in a place with so much cultural capital, there's at least a small contingent of good bookstores.

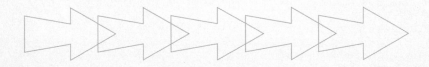

NEW YORK

LOS ANGELES

THE STRAND

828 Broadway,
New York, NY 10003

The iconic downtown bookshop just a short walk from NYU and Union Square overflows with its "miles and miles" of books.

BOOK SOUP

8818 Sunset Boulevard,
West Hollywood, CA 90069

Nuzzled among rock-and-roll venues like the Viper Room and Whisky A Go Go, this legendary bookstore in Los Angeles features an expansive selection of volumes, knowledgeable staff, and a distinctly Hollywood vibe.

MCNALLY JACKSON

52 Prince Street,
New York, NY 10012

Modern and refined bookstore with contemporary bestsellers and lots more in the hip, upscale SoHo neighborhood.

SKYLIGHT BOOKS

1818 N Vermont Avenue,
Los Angeles, CA 90027

Cozy and sleek store with contemporary bestsellers and lots more in a hip, upscale neighborhood.

BOOKS OF WONDER

18 W Eighteenth Street,
New York, NY 10011
217 W Eighty-Fourth Street,
New York, NY 10024

Featuring rows and rows of children's books, this indie bookstore, which has two locations, has become a premiere destination for readings and signings by acclaimed children's book authors.

CHILDREN'S BOOK WORLD

10580 1/2 W Pico Boulevard,
Los Angeles, CA 90064

With knowledgeable staff and shelves overflowing with titles, this large indie bookstore has become the best destination for children's lit on the West Coast.

SHOPPING

New York has Fifth Avenue, while Los Angeles has Rodeo Drive. Los Angeles has Santa Monica, while New York has SoHo. You can shop till you drop in either city, finding anything you need for any budget, style, or purpose. Yet to compare street by street—or store by store—feels a bit like a fool's errand as, unfortunately, shopping in cities across the globe have started to look more and more alike. Gap, Zara, Uniqlo, and the like can be found everywhere. What's there to compare? Beyond these standard chains, however, each city has its own collection of fantastic and original shopping centers, whether they be flea markets or malls.

FLEA MARKETS

GRAND BAAZAR

*100 W Seventy-Seventh Street,
New York, 10024*

The Upper West Side institution launched in 1983 as essentially a glorified yard sale to benefit local public schools, and it has since grown into one of the largest weekly markets in the city (and still maintains its mission).

ROSE BOWL FLEA

*1001 Rose Bowl Drive,
Pasadena, CA 91101*

More than 2,500 vendors and 20,000 visitors make up this Eastside institution, which runs on the second Sunday of every month (and has for more than forty-five years!).

HESTER STREET FAIR

*Essex Street,
New York, NY 10002*

Founded in 2010 with a distinct mission to support local artisans and makers, it attracts a cool, diverse, local crowd.

MELROSE TRADING POST

*7850 Melrose Avenue,
Los Angeles, CA 90046*

For more than twenty years, the West Hollywood location at Fairfax High School has been selling vintage treasures steps away from some of the hottest sneaker and streetwear stores in the city.

ARTISTS & FLEAS

Original location:
70 N Seventh Street,
Williamsburg,
Brooklyn, NY 11249

Popping up in the quickly gentrifying Brooklyn neighborhood in 2003, this hip artisanal market now has three locations across some of New York's hippest neighborhoods, where you can shop among some of the city's most stylish crowds.

SILVERLAKE FLEA

1511 Micheltorena Street,
Los Angeles, CA 90026

Once a month in the most hipster of neighborhoods, shop among some of the city's most stylish denizens.

HELL'S KITCHEN FLEA MARKET

W Thirty-Ninth Street
at Ninth Avenue,
New York, NY 10018

Operating since 1976, this flea features lots of high-end costume-style accessories and clothing, perhaps due to its proximity to Times Square.

TOPANGA VINTAGE MARKET

Victory Boulevard &
Mason Avenue,
Woodland Hills, CA 91306

Running on the fourth Sunday of every month, this flea focuses on vintage goods and has a decidedly old-school, hippie vibe.

BROOKLYN FLEA

*80 Pearl Street,
Brooklyn, NY 11201*

With two trendy Brooklyn locations, this popular flea features a variety of local artisans and curated, high-quality vintage goods in its chic DUMBO location.

SANTA MONICA AIRPORT OUTDOOR ANTIQUE & COLLECTIBLE MARKET

*Santa Monica Airport,
3223 Donald Douglas Loop S,
Santa Monica, CA 90405*

A bit of a higher-end market with lots of housewares and antiques from around the globe set in an airport hanger in the quaint Santa Monica Airport.

MALLS

THE SHOPS AT COLUMBUS CIRCLE

*10 Columbus Circle,
New York, NY 10019*

While it might technically be a mall, the offerings are so high-end and include one of the city's top restaurants (Per Se), it'll smash your prior conceptions of what it means to be a mall.

THE GROVE, AMERICANA AT BRAND, PALISADES VILLAGE, COMMONS AT CALABASAS

These shining gems of the Rick Caruso empire of outdoor shopping malls sprinkled across affluent Southern California neighborhoods and all featuring a focus on central public spaces, high-end shopping, and over-the-top holiday celebrations (like real snowfall in Southern California at the Grove!) will make you question whether you're even in a mall at all.

BROOKFIELD PLACE SHOPPING CENTER

*230 Vesey Street,
New York, NY 10281*

High-end retailers breathe life into this sleek and massive shopping center adjacent to the World Trade Center.

WESTFIELD CENTURY CITY

*10250 Santa Monica Boulevard,
Los Angeles, CA 90067*

The mall's original site dates back to 1964, but Westfield's ownership in the early aughts brought a newly redesigned concept that premiered in 2017 (along with the first West Coast Eataly).

WESTFIELD WORLD TRADE CENTER

*185 Greenwich Street,
New York, NY 10007*

Designed by world-renowned architect Santiago Calatrava, the eye-catching "Oculus" serves as the third-largest transportation hub in the city right at the base of the World Trade Center and 9/11 memorial. The stores within it are operated by Westfield and offer a solid mix of high-end stores and more typical chains.

THIRD STREET PROMENADE & SANTA MONICA PLACE

Third Street in downtown Santa Monica has been a shopping hub since the city's founding, but in the mid-1960s it converted officially into a pedestrian-only center. In 1980, a Frank Gehry–designed shopping center opened at the street's terminus closest to the Pier, but was overhauled again in 2007 by Mall of America architect Jon Jerde.

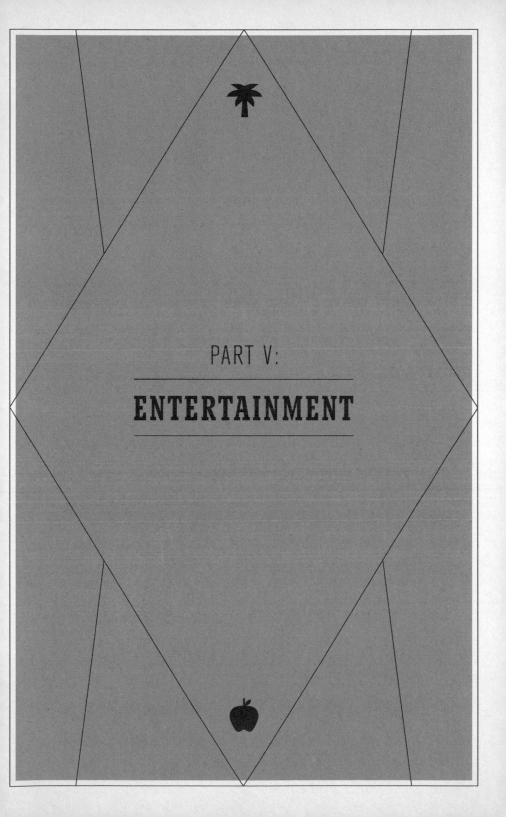

PART V:

ENTERTAINMENT

MUSIC

It's insane to think of all the music that spawned from—and now defines—New York: Simon & Garfunkel, Jennifer Lopez, Bob Dylan, Nas, Frank Sinatra, Lou Reed, Wu-Tang Clan, Madonna . . . the list goes on and on. But Los Angeles, too, has its equal share of musical giants: the Doors, Tupac, Dr. Dre, Kendrick Lamar, the Beach Boys, N.W.A., Guns N' Roses.

> **"In New York, concrete jungle where dreams are made of 'there's nothin' you can't do.' Now you're in New York. These streets will make you feel brand new. Big lights will inspire you. Let's hear it for New York, New York, New York."**

—"Empire State of Mind" by Jay-Z and Alicia Keys

> **"Sometimes I feel like my only friend is the city I live in, the City of Angels."**

—"Under the Bridge" by the Red Hot Chili Peppers

NEW YORK   ## LOS ANGELES

BEACON THEATRE

2124 Broadway,
New York, NY 10023

With 2,894 seats, this
vaudeville theater opened
in 1929 and was the site
of three early Tony Award
shows. It remains a
gorgeous example of
architecture of the period.

THE WILTERN

3790 Wilshire Boulevard,
Los Angeles, CA 90010

Opened in 1931, this historic
and refined example of art
deco architecture boasts a
cozy 1,850 seats.

MADISON SQUARE GARDEN

4 Pennsylvania Plaza,
New York, NY 10001

Known as MSG or the
Garden, this 20,000-plus-
seat massive arena hosts
shows for top-tier acts.

STAPLES CENTER

1111 S Figueroa Street,
Los Angeles, CA 90015

With 21,000 seats,
it's the crown jewel of
Los Angeles arenas.

YANKEE STADIUM

1 E 161st Street, Bronx,
New York, NY 10451

With a capacity of more
than 50,000, it's a legendary
outdoor arena for concerts
on an epic scale.

HOLLYWOOD BOWL

2301 N Highland Avenue,
Los Angeles, CA 90068

Since 1929 it has played host
to every famous act—and
with 17,500 seats nestled
into the Hills, it's somehow
both intimate and epic.

RADIO CITY MUSIC HALL

1260 Sixth Avenue,
New York, NY 10020

With a grand opening in 1932, the home of the Rockettes has stunning art deco architecture to complement its high-caliber musical acts.

GREEK THEATRE

2700 N Vermont Avenue,
Los Angeles, CA 90027

One of the best venues in the nation for live music due to its state-of-the-art acoustics, this 5,870-seat outdoor venue has held a place in Angelenos' hearts since 1930.

VILLAGE VANGUARD

178 Seventh Avenue S,
New York, NY 10014

This historic jazz club in the West Village opened in 1935 and has played host to numerous legendary acts, such as John Coltrane.

LIGHTHOUSE CAFE

30 Pier Avenue,
Hermosa Beach, CA 90254

One of the West Coast's premiere jazz clubs since 1949, it has played host to Miles Davis, Chet Baker, and Art Blakey and was featured in the film *La La Land.*

APOLLO THEATER

253 W 125th Street,
New York, NY 10027

The legendary Harlem venue opened in 1914 and has been a second home of sorts for a host of iconic performers as well as the site of the famous TV series *Showtime at the Apollo.*

EL REY THEATRE

5515 Wilshire Boulevard,
Los Angeles, CA 90036

It began as a first-run movie theater when it opened in 1936 but now hosts top-tier acts in an intimate art deco space.

KINGS THEATRE

1027 Flatbush Avenue,
Brooklyn, NY 11226

A classic art deco movie palace built in 1929, it sat dormant from the '70s until 2015, when it reopened to great acclaim.

TROUBADOUR

9081 N Santa Monica Boulevard,
West Hollywood, CA 90069

Having hosted Elton John's first US show in 1970, then becoming a second home for many of that generation's biggest acts, such as James Taylor and Joni Mitchell, it's a legendary club with a capacity of four hundred in West Hollywood.

SOB (SOUNDS OF BRAZIL)

204 Varick Street,
New York, NY 10014

One of the single-most legendary hip-hop clubs in the country.

THE WORLD STAGE

4321 Degnan Boulevard,
Los Angeles, CA 90008

This eclectic jazz club was founded in 1989 by renowned jazz drummer Billy Higgins and poet Kamau Daáood and features a wide range of music.

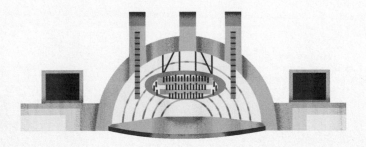

COMEDY CLUBS

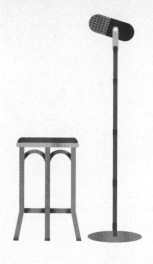

You've heard the stories about seeing Jerry Seinfeld or Chris Rock or any other massive comic when they were kids, doing sets at hole-in-the-wall bars to a half-dozen disinterested folks. But where are these fabled bars? Where can you find the best up-and-coming stand-up talent in New York and LA? And where can you go to see the top dogs?

NEW YORK

THE BELL HOUSE

149 Seventh Street,
Brooklyn, NY 11215

Located in Gowanus—the most Brooklyn-y neighborhood—this comedy club also features lots of live podcast recordings, readings of all types, and indie music acts in a converted printing press building.

LOS ANGELES

THE LARGO

366 N La Cienega Boulevard,
Los Angeles, CA 90048

An alternative comedy favorite in West Hollywood, it has hosted the likes of Tenacious D, the Dan Band, and Sarah Silverman.

CAROLINES ON BROADWAY

*1626 Broadway,
New York, NY 10019*

A top spot since 1981 in Times Square, the biggest names in comedy—including Jerry Seinfeld, Jay Leno, and *SNL* cast members—have all been known to perform here.

LAUGH FACTORY

*8001 Sunset Boulevard,
Los Angeles, CA 90046*

Now a chain, but one of the premiere spots in LA for some of the biggest acts.

COMEDY CELLAR

*117 MacDougal Street,
New York, NY 10012*

Open since 1982, it's thought of as one of the best comedy clubs in the world by many comedians.

THE COMEDY STORE

*8433 Sunset Boulevard,
Los Angeles, CA 90069*

An LA institution beloved by comics.

GOTHAM COMEDY CLUB

*208 W Twenty-Third Street,
New York, NY 10011*

One of the top clubs for big-name talent since 1996.

COMEDY UNION

*5040 Pico Boulevard,
Los Angeles, CA 90019*

The first black-owned and -operated comedy club in Los Angeles, playing host to a wide range of top-tier acts.

UCB THEATRE

555 W Forty-Second Street,
New York, NY 10009

Born out of an improv troupe in Chicago with now-famous members Amy Poehler, Mark Walsh, Adam McKay, Rick Roman, Horatio Sanz, Drew Franklin, and Matt Besser, the group moved to Chelsea in 1999 and since then have opened a second location in the Lower East Side. Still the premiere site for improv talent and a feeder for *SNL* and others.

THE GROUNDLINGS

7307 Melrose Avenue,
Los Angeles, CA 90046

A foundational improvisational theater where characters like Pee-wee Herman and Austin Powers were born.

UNION HALL

702 Union Street,
Brooklyn, NY, 11215

Home of the hipster, underground comedy scene.

THE VIRGIL

4519 Santa Monica Boulevard,
Los Angeles, CA 90029

Hipster, cool comedy on the Eastside of LA.

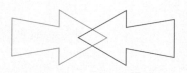

MOVIE THEATERS

Despite the fear and speculation that as Netflix continues on its path of world domination, movie theaters will be headed the way of the dinosaurs, there exists a handful of delightful, interesting, and enjoyable cinemas across both New York and Los Angeles. From historical theaters to contemporary shrines, you can find the perfect setting to enjoy a flick on either coast in no time.

NEW YORK

QUAD CINEMA

34 W Thirteenth Street,
New York, NY 10011

The city's first multiplex opened in 1972 in Greenwich Village, then underwent renovations between 2015 and 2017, opening again with a tailored, high-end design and adjacent bar.

METROGRAPH

7 Ludlow Street,
New York, NY 10002

A retro, lovingly designed theater by innovative director, writer, and designer Alexander Olch.

LOS ANGELES

THE THEATRE AT THE ACE HOTEL

929 S Broadway,
Los Angeles, CA 90015

This massive, 1,600-seat movie theater—built in the 1920s and bought and revitalized by the Ace Hotel—promises to give you one of the grandest movie experiences you'll ever have.

NEW BEVERLY CINEMA

7165 Beverly Boulevard,
Los Angeles, CA 90036

The single-screen cinema in midcity with programming from owner Quentin Tarantino.

ALAMO DRAFTHOUSE CINEMA

445 Albee Square West,
Brooklyn, NY 11201

The Austin, Texas, staple that's been serving craft beers with its indie programming since it opened in 2016.

ARCLIGHT

6360 W Sunset Boulevard,
Los Angeles, CA 90028

Opened in 1963, this Hollywood multiplex is popular with industry types and features the famed Cinerama Dome, a cutting-edge geodesic dome designed by Buckminster Fuller.

ANGELIKA FILM CENTER

18 W Houston Street
at Mercer Street,
New York, NY 10012

This independent movie stalwart downtown has been championing left-of-center films since 1989.

TCL CHINESE THEATRE IMAX

6925 Hollywood Boulevard,
Hollywood, CA 90028

If New York's most beloved theater is an indie darling, then Los Angeles's must be the epic king of scale and spectacle, the famed Chinese Theatre on Hollywood Boulevard.

COBBLE HILL CINEMAS

265 Court Street,
Brooklyn, NY 11231

The cute multiplex in Brooklyn's charming and chic Cobble Hill.

PARAMOUNT DRIVE-IN THEATER

7770 Rosecrans Avenue,
Paramount, CA 90723

Southern California's last remaining drive-in movie theater!

IFC

323 Sixth Avenue,
New York, NY 10014

The television network IFC took over the original Waverly Theater in 2005, which was the site of the original midnight screenings of the cult classic *Rocky Horror Picture Show.* The theater continues to cultivate an art-house vibe and roster to this day.

NUART THEATER

11272 Santa Monica
Boulevard, just west
of the 405 Freeway,
West Lost Angeles, CA 90025

The art house opened in 1929 in West LA and plays mainly art house films, but is most famous for its longtime run of *Rocky Horror Picture Show* every Saturday at midnight.

CINEMA VILLAGE

22 E Twelfth Street,
New York, NY 10003

A tiny, old-school cinema right off of University Place, steps from NYU in Greenwich Village.

VISTA THEATRE

4473 Sunset Drive,
Los Angeles, CA 90027

An itty-bitty, quirky, old-school cinema in the heart of Silver Lake.

THE PARIS THEATER

4 W Fifty-Eighth Street,
New York, NY 10019

Manhattan's only remaining single-screen cinema, which gives its screened movies an air of importance, much like a stage play.

AERO THEATRE

1328 Montana Avenue,
Santa Monica, CA 90403

A cute single-screen cinema on Santa Monica's Montana Avenue in one of its most charming and chic locations.

ACKNOWLEDGMENTS

This book is the result of a fun little idea that snowballed into a concept only after many hours of discussion and debate with my family and friends. It would not have been possible without you.

I especially would like to thank my parents for rearing me in Los Angeles and for their inspiration and unwavering support in everything I do. My sister and brother, as well as my extended family, for their love and support. My friends for their ideas, opinions, and our endless debates about food, music, and, well, everything else, all of which proved to (finally!) be useful for something in writing this book. Most importantly, thank you to my wife, who drew me to New York for the first and second times and who finally agreed to move to the West Coast.

I also want to thank the entire team that helped make this book possible, including my agents, Megan Thompson and Cindy Uh, and everyone at Running Press, including most especially my editor Jess Riordan, illustrator Sol Linero, designer Jenna McBride, copy editor Susan Hom, proofreader Josephine Moore, publicist Amy Cianfrone, and editorial director Jennifer Kasius.

I have included a list of important sources researched in the bibliography to follow, but I want to make special mention to the following websites that I went back to time and time again: *Condé Nast Traveler*, Curbed, Culinary Lore, Discover Los Angeles, Eater,

First We Feast, *Food 52*, *Food and Wine Magazine*, Frommers, the *Hollywood Reporter*, Infatuation, LaFoodie.com, *Los Angeles Magazine*, Mental Floss, ModernHiker.com, *New York Magazine*, the *New York Times*, *The New Yorker*, Thrillist, Time Out, and Untapped Cities. All incredible and worth checking out.

BIBLIOGRAPHY

Arbeiter, M. "15 Fascinating Facts About the Brooklyn Bridge," *Mental Floss*, 24 May 2018, http://mentalfloss.com/article/68463/15-facts-about-brooklyn-bridge-you-wont-fuhgeddaboud

Arellano, Gustavo. *Taco USA: How Mexican Food Conquered America*. New York: Scribner, 2012.

Balinska, Maria. *The Bagel: The Surprising History of a Modest Bread*. Cornwall: Yale University Press, 2009.

Baum, Gary. "Chefs Michael Voltaggio and Eddie Huang Debate L.A. vs. N.Y. Cuisine: Fine Dining, Fast Food and Customers," *Hollywood Reporter*, 12 April 2016, https://www.hollywoodreporter.com/news/chefs-michael-voltaggio-eddie-huang-880639

Bhabha, Leah. "The History of Sushi in the U.S.," *Food 52*, 29 November 2013, https://food52.com/blog/9183-the-history-of-sushi-in-the-u-s

Brightwell, Eric. https://ericbrightwell.com

Butler, Stephanie, "A Rare History of the Steakhouse," *History*, 24 October 2014, https://www.history.com/news/a-rare-history-of-the-steakhouse

Butler, Stephanie, "Nigiri to California Rolls: Sushi in America," *History*, 12 December 2014, https://www.history.com/news/nigiri-to-california-rolls-sushi-in-america

Chandler, Jenna. "Which LA Neighborhood Do You Really Live In?" *Curbed LA*, 22 June 2018, http://la.curbed.com/2017/7/28/16059422/los-angeles-neighborhoods-map

Chiland, Ellijah. "Did a Conspiracy Really Destroy LA's Huge Streetcar System?" *Curbed LA*, 26 January 2018, https://la.curbed.com/2017/9/20/16340038/los-angeles-streetcar-conspiracy-theory-transit-mythgeneral-motors

Dai, Serena and Stefanie Tuder. "The Classic Steakhouses of New York City," *Eater NY*, 27 November 2018, https://ny.eater.com/maps/best-nyc-steakhouse-classic

Darling, Michael. "A Brief History of Hollywood Sign Pranks," *LAist*, 3 April 2017, https://laist.com/2017/04/03/hollywood_sign_pranks.php

Esparza, Bill. "The 38 Essential Tacos in Los Angeles," *Eater LA*, 27 April 2018, https://la.eater.com/maps/best-tacos-los-angeles-taquerias-mexican

Godoy, Maria, "Lo Mein Loophole: How U.S. Immigration Law Fueled a Chinese Restaurant Boom," *NPR*, 22 February 2016, https://www.npr.org/sections/thesalt/2016/02/22/467113401/lo-mein-loophole-how-u-s-immigration-law-fueled-a-chinese-restaurant-boom

Gordinier, Jeff, "Making Vegan a New Normal," *New York Times*, 24 September 2012, https://www.nytimes.com/2012/09/26/dining/vegan-food-is-in-mainstream-in-southern-california.html

Harris, Karen, "Fast Food Drive-Thru: A Product of the Car Culture," *History Daily*, 24 September 2018, http://historydaily.org/fast-food-drive-thru-a-product-of-the-car-culture

Hayoun, Massoud, "This Is America's Best Chinese Food," *Explore Parts Unknown*, 4 April 2017, https://explorepartsunknown.com/koreatown-la/san-gabriel-valley-chinese-food/

"History of San Francisco's Chinatown," *History*, https://www.history.com/topics/immigration/san-francisco-chinatown

Joe, Elaine. "The Story of Chinatown," *PBS*, https://www.pbs.org/kqed/chinatown/resourceguide/story.html

Kang, Matthew, "The Source: LA's First Spiritual Vegetarian Restaurant," *Eater LA*, 13 May 2013, https://la.eater.com/2013/5/13/6435783/the-source-las-first-spiritual-vegetarian-restauran

Kral, Georgia and Nicole Levy, "Oldest Restaurants in NYC: Delmonico's, P.J. Clarke's, Katz's and More," *AM New York*, 6 July 2018, https://www.amny.com/eat-and-drink/old-restaurants-nyc-1.19634651

Kreuzer, Nikki. "The Oldest Surviving Los Angeles Restaurants... A Master List of the Vintage, Historic and Old School," *Offbeat LA*, 10 May 2015, https://the-losangelesbeat.com/2015/05/offbeat-l-a-the-oldest-surviving-los-angeles-restaurants-amaster-list-of-the-vintage-historic-and-old-school/

"LA's Best Drive Thrus," *L.A. Foodie*, http://lafoodie.com/post/34667640142/las-best-drive-thrus

Levine, Ed. "State of the Slice, Part 1: A Slice of New York Pizza History," *Serious Eats*, https://www.seriouseats.com/2018/10/new-york-pizza-slice-history.html

Loc, Tim. "Check Out This Amazing Map That Features Every L.A. Neighborhood," *LAist*, https://laist.com/2017/07/27/neighborhood_maps.php

Lohman, Sarah, "A Brief History of Sushi in the United States," *Mental Floss*, 3 March 2017, http://mentalfloss.com/article/92861/brief-history-sushi-united-states

Merwin, Ted. *Pastrami on Rye: An Overstuffed History of the Jewish Deli.* New York: NYU Press, 2015.

Nimoy, Leonard. "Press Release From the Griffith Observatory," 19 March 2001, http://www.spaceref.com/news/viewpr.html?pid=4402

Novak, Matt. "Nobody Walks in L.A.: The Rise of Cars and the Monorails That Never Were," *Smithsonian*, 26 April 2013, https://www.smithsonianmag.com/history/nobody-walks-in-la-the-rise-of-cars-and-the-monorails-that-never-were-43267593/

Pines, Giulia. "From Bad to Wurst: The Real Story of German Deli Meats," *Vice*, 8 August 2014, https://munchies.vice.com/en_us/article/vvxyw3/from-bad-to-wurst-the-real-story-of-german-deli-meats

Reichl, Ruth. "For Red Meat and a Sense of History," *New York Times*, 21 January 1994, https://www.nytimes.com/1994/01/21/arts/for-red-meat-and-a-sense-of-history.html

Sax, David. *Save the Deli: In Search of Perfect Pastrami, Crusty Rye, and the Heart of Jewish Delicatessen*. New York: Mariner Press, 2010.

Schwarz, Benjamin and Christina Schwarz. "Going All Out for Chinese," *The Atlantic*, January 1999, https://www.theatlantic.com/magazine/archive/1999/01/going-all-out-for-chinese/305473/

Shields, Tim. "How to Photograph the Back of the Hollywood Sign," *PetaPixel*, 01 October 2018, https://petapixel.com/2018/10/01/how-to-photograph-the-back-of-the-hollywood-sign/

Siemaszko, Corky. "How Emily Warren Roebling Helped Save—and Complete—the Brooklyn Bridge," *New York Daily News*, 24 May 2012, https://www.nydailynews.com/new-york/brooklyn/emily-warren-roebling-helped-save-completebrooklyn-bridge-article-1.1083976

Smith, Steve and Sharon Steel. "The 50 Best Songs About New York," *Time Out*, 3 November 2016, https://www.timeout.com/newyork/music/best-songs-about-new-york

Solares, Nick, "The Story of Papaya King, a New York City Original," *Eater NY*, 16 July 2015, https://ny.eater.com/cheap-eats/2015/7/16/8955961/papaya-king

"Sushi in America," *Food & Wine*, 16 June 2017, https://www.foodandwine.com/articles/sushi-in-america

T, Eric, "Was McDonald's the First Fast Food Chain to Use Drive-Thru Windows?," *Culinary Lore*, 20 April 2016, https://culinarylore.com/food-history:was-mcdonalds-first-to-use-drive-thru-window/

Viguet, Meridith, "Papaya King and Gray's Papaya: When Did Papayas and Hot Dogs Become an NYC Trend?" *Untapped Cities*, 28 October 2013, https://untappedcities.com/2013/10/28/papaya-king-grays-papaya-when-did-papayas-hot-dogs-become-nyc-trend/

Watt, Alex. "The Original Location of 30 Food Chains," *Mental Floss*, 24 July 2015, http://mentalfloss.com/article/60877/original-locations-30-famous-food-chains

Wei, Clarissa, "How LA Became a Powerhouse for Chinese Food," *First We Feast*, 20 January 2015, https://firstwefeast.com/eat/2015/01/how-l-a-became-a-powerhouse-for-chinese-food

Wetheimer, Kate and Michael Juliano. "The 50 Best Songs About Los Angeles," *Time Out*, 3 August 2014, https://www.timeout.com/los-angeles/music/the-50-best-la-songs